HELP US O GOD

To Seek Supernatural Faith ● *To Avoid Evil Example*

HELP US O GOD

We Need Help in Our Troubled World

FATHER BEDE REYNOLDS, O.S.B.

ALBA BOOKS

CANFIELD, OHIO 44406

Imprimi Potest

+ Eugene Medved, O.S.B.
Abbot of Westminster Abbey

Nihil Obstat

Daniel J. Carey, D.P.
Censor Librorum

Imprimatur

+ Most Rev. James F. Carney, D.D.
Archbishop of Vancouver

ISBN: 0-8189-1162-X

Library of Congress Catalog Card Number: 80-65720

© Copyright 1980, Alba House Communications
Canfield, OHIO 44406

Printed in the United States of America

To Our Lady — Mother of God's Church

MAY SHE

"Direct and order all my
doings in accordance with the
will of her only Son"

FOREWORD

AN ESTIMATE OF LIFE

BASED ON TWENTY-FIVE YEARS OF EXPERIENCE AS A BENEDICTINE PRIEST MONK

First and last let me say that the life of every single individual creature possessed of intelligence and will, is the best possible result of every quarter-second of that life that God, in His infinite love, could achieve without compulsion of the will of that individual creature. And that is true of Satan and the Archangel Gabriel. It is true of every saint and of every soul in hell.

The setting in which each life is lived is the best possible setting in which God, in His infinite love, could make available for that life without compulsion of the will of any individual whose acts have affected that setting since the beginning of time, other than the physical events which have all been managed by God with infinite perfection since the beginning of time. The obstacles in any setting caused by present scandals or past evil are minutely managed by God so that, while each individual life is different at every moment from every other life that has ever been lived, sainthood is available to every single individual who will unite his or her will in partnership with God. And God will manage everything to the extent that He is allowed.

To substantiate this notion, here is a quote of the words of Christ to the mystic, Gabrielle Bossis, on September 12, 1940, as reported in the little book, *He & I*, published by Editions Paulines of Sherbrooke, Quebec:

"Oh! this desire of My eternal love for oneness. I begin My life on earth again with each one of you—My life wedded to yours—if you want to invite Me. You remem-

Foreword

ber how I walked with the disciples of Emmaus? . . . I do this for you. I walk along the same path with you, the path I chose for you from all eternity—in this family, in this country where you live. It is I who placed you there with a special love. So live there, full of faith, remembering that that is where you will win heaven, where you will win eternal love for this brief moment of time . . . So pass through this life with the great desire to respond to all my tenderness and with constant impatience to know Me at last—to know Me, your loving Savior. Haven't you always been a thought in My eternal mind? It would be only just for yours to be filled with Me, My poor little children, so often ungrateful."

Then, *second and in between:* Let me say that the life of a Priest or a Religious, lived in partnership with God, is by all odds the most precious vocation there is in this world. Here again, every such life is different from every other life that has ever been lived and each is minutely designed by Christ to accomplish exactly the most perfect result that He can manage without compelling the will of that individual.

And, to express it in another way, let me quote from a letter I wrote to the Editor of *Leaves* magazine of Jan.-Feb. 1976:

"After thirty years as an "Older Man For Christ," I would like to tell the readers of *Leaves* that if the Catholic men who become widowers had even the vaguest notion of the preciousness of the Catholic priesthood, our monasteries and seminaries would be jammed with long waiting lists of those seeking to crown happy married life by dedication of the remainder of their lives to God.

It has always amazed me that so very few realize this truth. There is no possible future for one who becomes a widow or widower which could compare with the life of a religious or a priest."

And to make all this easy, I know of no better formula than that which I have stated on page 52 of my book, *Let's Mend the Mess!*

> "I am at last beginning to learn what I should have known all the time, and what I want the reader to gain more quickly than I have—that God is always available, in fact, right in one's heart! He is there with all His power and all His love, ready for you to turn to Him at the slightest need and with such intimacy that it is as if you were the only soul that had such a privilege.
>
> There may be temptations to sin; there may be temptations to doubt; there may be events which at first seem impossible to attribute to God's love. But Faith says "NO"! And God is immediately present to back that Faith with grace which will turn back every temptation, settle every doubt, survive every trial— provided we remember God's presence constantly and turn to Him quickly and trust Him completely.
>
> And so it will always be, in every trial, in every formidable assignment, in every brush with a different situation, in every temptation, God will prove His promise made through the Psalmist: 'I keep the Lord always in my sight; since He is at my right hand I shall not be moved. Therefore my heart rejoices and my soul is glad; even my body will rest secure.'" (Ps. 15:8-9).

God has made all this so obvious in my own life as to make a statement of it sound trite. I have recorded it all before but it has unwound in a legacy that so clinches the certainty that it has been God's doing, that it is worth a little repetition to tie it all together.

The maneuvering that led to my being drafted as a blind date to meet my future wife one week after transferring from Cornell University to the University of California and the circumstances that brought about that meeting, furnish par excellence an example of God's planning impossible to interpret in any other way.

Foreword

Then, the fact that she turned out to be a saint who could undo and re-do my whole spiritual mentality, even though it took her twenty-one years to do it, is even more convincing. Then the dear old Paulist Father who, in twenty-one days made us both daily Communicants, is only incidental to the supreme end of it all which only God could have brought about in exactly the manner it *was* brought about. He made me a Benedictine Priest Monk with a background of improbability sufficiently definite and interesting and amusing to cause my Superior to give me the command to put it in writing in the form of the conversion story, *A Rebel from Riches.*

Next, by placing me just over the border line in Canada, God made it necessary for me to return to the United States for six months to avoid double Income Tax on the liquidating trust estate of my possessions. That brought about the start of a series of conferences to my Catholic and non-Catholic friends in Pasadena, California, which had been my home for fifty-two years.

And *that* made me eligible when a phone call came to Father Abbot at ten o'clock one evening from the Superior at Cenacle Retreat House in Vancouver, to be assigned to give a retreat starting the following afternoon. The fact that that retreat was a success after such short notice led to other assignments for twenty odd other retreats.

The result has been that I have prepared about one hundred and thirty half-hour conferences which gave material for four more books and also gave me a perspective which I have tried to put into the pages that follow and present as *a legacy of twenty-five years as a Benedictine Priest Monk.*

CONTENTS

CHAPTER	PAGE
Foreword	vii
1 Deliver Us From Evil	1
2 What Are We Here For	11
3 A New Pentecost in the Souls of Men	23
4 Daily Mass—The Source of Power	35
5 God's Law and Man's Law	45
6 Thy Will Be Done	58
7 Fools' Gold and Project Sainthood	68
8 More Blessed Receivers	77
9 Our Father Who Art in Heaven	86
10 Jesus Christ Our Lord	96
11 Face Danger With Mary	106
12 Danger and Vocations	120
13 Danger and the Vocation of Marriage	131
14 Ecclesiam Suam Warns of Danger	141
15 Charity Shields From Danger	151
16 A Message to Everyone — *Addressed to Divorced Catholic Women*	163
17 God's Love Offers Peace and Joy to Everybody	175

CHAPTER I
DELIVER US FROM EVIL

It has been suggested that I follow up my *"Five Man Team of Books"* aimed at *mending the mess in the world and in the Church,* with a brief survey of business, comparing 1926, when I ended my active business career, with 1976, which Father Tom Mooney of El Paso, Texas, characterizes as "An Age In Rebellion Against Itself." The suggestion asked for comment on the decline in ethics, the immorality endemic to business, business and religion, business and politics, business and weapons of war, etc., etc.

I have done a lot of thinking along these lines and heartily agree that these items are desperately in need of consideration by every human being as we enter the 1980's.

My graduation from the University of California in December, 1914, as a Bachelor of Science in Civil Engineering, coincided approximately with the full scale devastation of World War One in Europe. My career in business began on June 1st, 1915, as timekeeper in a plant madly producing the ingredients of high-octane gasoline to meet the needs of a world plunging ever deeper into the turmoil of that war. My withdrawal from the same business, many times enlarged, in 1926, with more money than I had ever dreamed of owning, could reasonably be assumed to place me in the category of the vastly increasing company of so-called sophisticates who credit science with all the necessary answers of life.

Then, having spent sixteen years, at least outwardly, in that category, World War Two called me back into the Los Angeles office of the Gasoline Division of the Petroleum Administration for War in a position where I represented the Government in its dealings with all of the executives concerned with the production of "natural gasoline" exactly as I had been sixteen years earlier. I think it is fair to say that I was in a prime position to observe the characteristics of that particular section of business at that particular time.

During my first few weeks in that position I was amazed and perplexed by the many changes which seemed to have left me utterly disqualified to carry on in dealings with men in positions such as I had occupied before. Two characteristics of these changes left me in dismay. In these brief sixteen years the advance in technology had given the industry a vocabulary that made me a stranded foreigner when they talked business and, still more devastating to me, it seemed that the atmosphere of business ethics had created a code where it was "Every man for himself and the Devil take the hindermost."

The first item of these changes cost me many hours of "midnight oil" coupled with recourse to old friends who could coach me in secret till I could finally talk their language. The second item, I finally came to see as a phase of world-thinking which yields to influences characteristic of fallen man. I feel certain that if I should go back into the same business now, after three times sixteen years, it would still more emphatically exhibit these influences which lie at the base of human behavior.

Of all these influences which mould man's behavior, two stand out as unique since they control man's relations to all other influences. The first influence is all-embracing and is of the very essence of human behavior. It is the existence of *the supernatural*. The second is merely the characteristic of human nature that man is largely influenced in his decisions by the *example* of others.

The history of the human race has shown quite definitely the overwhelming mastery of these two influences. Weak or absent supernatural faith has generated bad example. Wholesale bad example has sucked in the unthinking until amoral behavior has scuttled the welfare of society in every direction. The decline in business ethics and the misuse of money and the sinful pursuit of wealth are only items or symptoms of this devastating decay which invites and eventually will produce a colossal crash and an enforced return to sanity and even to spiritual regeneration.

It is my belief and hope that, instead of relating the harrowing details of one branch of human misbehavior, it will be far more useful to shout the *danger of disaster* and seek to avoid that disaster by showing the *necessity* of Supernatural Faith and the utter folly of accepting bad example.

Before discussing these influences further, it is absolutely necessary to explain exactly what is meant by the phrase, "the necessity of Supernatural Faith." The word "supernatural" itself needs immediate clarification. The etymology of the adjective, supernatural, fits precisely with its meaning, i.e. being above that which is born or created as is the visible and observable universe. But before elaborating that meaning it is most important to rid the word of a sort of spooky connotation which it has been given in modern language. The true meaning of the word has absolutely nothing to do with that which we think of as magic or occult.

The supernatural, used as a noun means: All that is perceived beyond sense-perception which invites belief in the *necessity* of a Source of all that is observable by man's natural senses. It is the evidence of the necessity of an infinite, all-wise, all-powerful Being demanded by the fact of the universe. Man's gift of intelligence gives him access to the perception of the supernatural. And *Supernatural Faith* is the acceptance of this perception and all the infinitely precious treasure that this acceptance makes available to man's soul.

It may seem that I have been very devious in my explanation of the supernatural instead of referring immediately to its relationship to God. There is, however, a reason. Supernatural Faith, far removed from any connotation of magic, is the all-important determinant of man's behavior. The object of Supernatural Faith is the one and only concrete, one-hundred per cent self-existent *Reality* that IS. All else is held in being from moment to moment by the will and the power of that *Reality*.

That is a flat statement of fact supported by an infinite abundance of two kinds of evidence, either one of which is adequate. It flatly denies the theory of the Atheist which he holds because he has willed to close his mind to both kinds of evidence. He bases his denial on the unsupported choice of his will which has no alternative but to claim the self-existence of all that is, in the face of billions of statistics which show it to be impossible. Furthermore, he has not one example to give proof that anything has ever come into being by its own volition.

The reason that there is no compulsion to cancel the atheist denial stems from the nature of the Triune Personal Being who IS. He has no dependence upon creation but has created this universe with one purpose in view—to provide Himself with creatures capable of sharing the enjoyment of His infinite perfection. That means creatures equipped with the utterly amazing capacity to *know* and to *love*. But that isn't even the half of it.

It was easy for God to create such creatures. But it was the *use* of that capacity by this creature in the manner intended by God, that shaped God's plan of creation. And the manner of that use intended by God was that it should be absolutely free from compulsion. In other words, the all-but-infinite time that God has used in the preparation and execution of His plan has been to provide a stage whereon this creature equipped with intelligence and will *can* come to know God and *can* love Him, by choice to be sure, but without compulsion! And that accounts for the world exactly as it is and its history exactly as it is, including the "Problem of Evil" exactly as it is and all that goes with it until the end of time. That, however, is not to say that God compelled or now compels the "Problem of Evil" to exist. And that requires a little further explanation about God.

The very first thing to say about God is that He IS infinite power, infinite wisdom, infinite love! and *that* all adds up to Infinite Perfection. God *cannot* make a mistake or do anything less than perfectly because He knows all the answers before the questions arise.

The infinite perfection of all that He has done or is doing or will do goes far beyond our ability to even comprehend it. It involves every quarter second of time from the beginning of creation throughout eternity. It also involves the behavior of every atom in every creature of the universe.

I often think of a way to emphasize that statement by one tiny finite example. God has given man the wonderful capacity to see, feel, hear, taste and smell. The sense of sight is perhaps the most wonderful of all. The mechanism and functioning of the human eye is all too easy for us who see to take for granted with little thought. But in fact it is an ever-living miracle of perfection that gives us, in accurate detail, the vision of all that surrounds us. Science tells us that some fourteen different functions must cooperate and coordinate to bring an image into being in our consciousness! What could more definitely shout an invitation to admit the *necessity* of a Creator than this precious possession of the power to see?

And yet, the Atheist is required to tell us that self-existent light, shining for trillions of years on self-existent living pieces of matter, has produced reactions within them that gradually found each other and one by one produced the fourteen capacities to function and eventually become an organ of sight. That may seem far-fetched but in reality every atom in every grain of sand is just as demanding of an answer as is the precious sense of sight. And infinitely more demanding still is the colossal aggregate of miracles of existence in ourselves and the world around us.

Saint Thomas Aquinas has sorted out these items of evidence into his famous five groups of proofs of the existence of the Creator which constitute a prodigious invitation to believe.

And what, it may be asked, are we invited to believe? The answer is indeed amazing! It is this: We and all that is, form the current stage in the fulfillment of God's infinite eternal plan to people heaven with creatures disciplined to perfect holiness and capacity to love, by their sojourn in the world exactly as it is.

We laugh over Eleanor Hodgman's irrepressibly optimistic "Pollyanna" and express the wish that we could live in her "best possible world." And it is right at this point that we reach the climax of all that I have written thus far. This *is* not only the best possible world, but it is the absolutely *perfect* world to accomplish the purpose for which God has made it. The infinite complex of evidence which we have been discussing invites us to believe that it is a contradiction in logic to assume that an infinitely wise, infinitely powerful God could pursue His purpose less than perfectly.

Deliver Us From Evil

But how can I be sure of all this in direct contradiction of the claim of the Atheists who seem to be on the way to becoming a large percentage of mankind? And that question brings up the final consideration of the two sources of *Supernatural Faith.*

The evidence of the material universe brings to the attention of the intelligence of man a potent invitation to read in that evidence the truth as I have described it. The response to that invitation from those throughout all history who have had no access to any other evidence, has varied all the way from practically perfect acceptance, to the flat denial held by Atheism.

And because that is true, and because the whole truth is almost beyond man's capacity to understand, God has provided a Revelation of the truth, both natural and supernatural, by direct communication exactly suited to the needs of each individual soul. It started in the experience of the first man and woman of the human race and has continued with infinite variation in form until the present day. All of it has been exactly suited to the legitimate need of our finite minds for a boost to the will to take that little step demanded by God to *give* Him that *trust* which, if compelled by self-love, would be detestable to God.

The climax of this Revelation is, of course, contained in the thirty-odd years spent among men by the Second Person of the Holy Triune God as the man Jesus of Nazareth. The manner of His sojourn on earth is the most amazing feature of all revelation. Here, again, it can be seen as the all-but-unbelievable exhibition of the immensity of His love *or* it can be called an impossibility that the God who has been described to us would do such a thing, even if He could!

Be that as it may, the Man Jesus did teach His

disciples a body of truth, and did establish an agency to project that body of truth in a manner which He said would be protected by His presence in their souls until the end of time. His acts and words were such that those who saw and heard them were willing to face torture and death rather than accept the inducement to deny Him. And there the evidence stands before all men of the present day, precisely fashioned by God to meet His claim that it is "sufficient", but never brought before any individual soul in a manner which would compel self-love to seek acceptance.

And there it stands. There is Revelation and there is the evidence available to science. God has brought it all about precisely as it is for a perfect reason. He asks for that little act of acceptance from the will of each human being. Until that act of *trust* in God's word is given, each one of us is subject to the hopeless bafflement of conflicting opinions and conflicting examples of behavior.

But it is a fact of experience that has no proof *but* experience, that God stands ready with the help that we call *Grace* which absolutely clinches the whole concept. When one can say: "My God, I believe. Help Thou my unbelief!" and mean it in the most inmost depth of his soul, God does clinch his Faith. And from there-on-in, God provides a perfect answer to every question of the soul by means of the *Grace of Faith—a supernatural gift*—and the Deposit of *Truth* as taught by Christ to His Apostles.

I have staked my life on the supernatural reality of the Promises of Christ. They furnish me with complete assurance of knowing what God has revealed. I do not mean by that, that I expect the guidance of my behavior to be automatic and free from responsibility on my part. I do, however, believe that we have God's guarantee of the peace and welfare of all men *if* and to the extent that men will put their trust in Him and be guided by the teaching that Christ brought to the world.

The present chaos of evil has been possible only because God's whole plan demands that He leave the will of man free to refuse His love. This can and will go on to complete disaster unless there will arise a wholesale *example* of turning back to God. It is to plead for this *example* that I wish to turn men's thoughts.

The overwhelming lust for *money* is the chief obstacle opposing that end. This recalls the words of Christ to the mystic, Gabrielle Bossis, as reported in that excellent pair of books, *He and I*. He says: "You know what is My enemy? *Money*. People think only of *Money*. They live for it and nothing else. And it hardens the heart without filling it." (Editions Paulines Sherbrooke, P.Q. 7-1-'48).

And it is just here that the utterly pitiful state of the Atheist and the doubter need our help and our prayer, since only God can remedy their plight.

Human respect, perhaps coupled with some degree of malice, prevents that little humble act of the will that opens the door to grace. I have experienced the grace that God gives in answer to that act of the will when it is genuine. The doubter might say to himself: "Let's just try this out and see what God will do." He might even say: "I believe" and try to mean it. But God reads hearts. He is right in the heart even of the Atheist and He knows the intention of the will. As long as the doubter asks God to *prove* what I have been telling you, God will not respond any more than He would respond to the quest of the taunter who said: "Let Him come down from the Cross and we will believe in Him!" How very tiny is the difference between my act and his. But his leaves him stranded and hopeless whether he admits it or not; mine gives me certain knowledge of the truth that I would not trade for all the money in the world.

And there the situation stands today! God offers *the Grace of Supernatural Faith* to every man, woman and child in the world. His way of offering it demands a tiny act of the will to open the door to God's Grace. There seems to be a growing percentage of those who refuse God that act of the will. The *example* of their behavior invites fallen-man to discount the *necessity* of acceptance. Until a way can be found to offset the attraction of that example there is grave DANGER for the souls of men!

To my mind, the comparison of business morality in 1926 and 1976 would simply be to amplify the assertion that *danger* exists. So I ask you to share with me a study of the means of offsetting the *example of evil* which is blinding all too many theologians, priests and people from the light of *true Supernatural Faith* in the means provided by God for our salvation.

CHAPTER II

WHAT ARE WE HERE FOR?

Some time ago I was given an assignment to preach a Lenten Conference on the subject: "Marriage, Family and Vocations." That subject can be made to lend itself to my theme: *God Manages Everything Perfectly*. And it also invites the warning of *danger* as a result of *waning Supernatural Faith* making souls vulnerable to *wholesale evil example*. So, to study that warning in the light of the *perfection* of God's Reign, I will call the title of this chapter: *What Are We Here For?* The answer to that question as applied to family life can, I believe, give us sound warning of a grave *danger* to be avoided.

And to put that thought into immediate action, I want to make a few categorical assertions and then defend them. The first one is this: Any Catholic who really understands the treasure of his Faith and commits himself wholeheartedly to it, can be absolutely free from anxiety, no matter what comes to pass in the Church or in the world today. Furthermore, that covers all that needs to be said to insure the success of marriage, perfect family life and plenty of vocations.

But just for fun, I will put a couple more markers on our path. Perhaps the most important of these markers is that most of what is wrong in the Church, the family, marriage, and vocations is the result of vicious scandal. And in using the word "scandal" I refer to its technical definition which is: that which leads others into sin or error as a result of one's words or acts. And this kind of scandal goes beyond sin and error by snowballing erroneous opinions to the point where doubt and anxiety ruin the welfare of souls.

And that is certainly where we stand today. But

before I begin to elaborate these statements, there is one more that I want to add that applies particularly to family well-being. It is this: The so-called generation-gap or age-gap is a deadly figment of the snowball of scandal that blights our age. Parents and children have indeed a very different atmosphere to live in but that need not change their relationship one iota if it is properly understood.

So, let us go back to our foundation question and ask: *What are we here for?* There is one answer which can quench all our anxiety about the modern world and the modern Church. It is, that we are here for a one-hundred-per-cent supernatural reason which is one-hundred-per-cent invisible to our senses. It is perceived by faith alone and that is a one-hundred-per-cent supernatural gift from God. We are made eligible for that gift, however, by acceptance of the evidence which God has furnished, of a Revelation which explains everything.

This evidence is very plain and easy to understand but it is set aside by billions of people in the world today. The Revelation is about a supernatural relationship between God and ourselves. A snowballing misinterpretation of the findings of material science can crush that little humble act of the will to *trust* in God. But that is what He asks of us to clinch for us the gift of faith in His Revelation.

The revelation is this (to condense a whole volume of catechism into one paragraph): The omnipotent, infinite, Triune God has created this universe and placed us in it in order to produce and train angelic and human creatures fit to live with Him and with each other forever in perfect love. God's method of training for this result is, however, utterly beyond our human understanding because it involves sin, suffering, poverty, the machinations of Satan, the Incarnation and Crucifixion of God Himself, and right now, the snowball of atheistic scandal propaganda that tends to quench all trust in the supernatural.

There is a part of this Revelation which invites our natural trust. It tells us that God, during His Incarnation in the world, provided for the continuation of our access to Him until the end of time. And that is accomplished by means of His Church which gives us constant supernatural contact with Him.

It is here today just as it has always been and always will be. It has always been battered by the snowball of scandal in denial of the supernatural in its make-up or denial of individual items of its teaching. But it continues to invite trust in God's guarantee of the infallible integrity of its Teaching Authority. This resides today in our Holy Father, Pope John Paul II and in his College of Bishops.

It is the penetration of this snowball of denial of the supernatural into the hearts of all too many priests and nuns and parents and children that is responsible for the drop-outs, the defections, the detestable disobedience to the Holy Father, the failure of marriages, the breach between parents and their children and all the rest of man's inhumanity to man.

And please do not think that I am innocently unaware of the tremendous pressures which reinforce the snowball. Nor is this a Pollyanna whoopee proclaiming that all is well with the world. But I hope it helps to explain what I meant in my first categorical assertion that any Catholic who really understands the treasure of his Faith and commits himself wholeheartedly to it, can be absolutely free from anxiety no matter what comes to pass in the Church or in the world today.

And I really mean that phrase: "no matter what comes to pass." The one thing I know *won't* happen is the thing that many of the dissidents claim *has* happened—false doctrine taught by the Holy Father or one of his predecessors. Why do I know it won't happen? Because of my supernatural certainty of the promise of God to the contrary.

Last year I gave a retreat to the seminarians at our Diocesan Seminary of Christ the King. On the final day one of my confreres reported to me a two-word comment made by one of the retreatants. It pleased me more than would pages of approval of the matter of the conferences. His words were: *What conviction!* And that puts the whole thing in a nutshell.

Another of my confreres remarked: "You can't afford to doubt your faith; you've got too much invested in it!" It is true that I have staked my whole life on the truth of God's revelation and God's promises. I only wish that I could put everybody else in the world in the same bind! I placed that stake forty-five years ago when I joined the Church and I made it binding with a Vow of Poverty thirty years ago. I wouldn't take back a dime of it today, *come what may.*

Let's see what all this adds up to. I now have in my file, correspondence regarding six broken marriages. Every one of the spouses is a lovable Catholic person. Not one of these marriages would have gone amok had there been a true supernatural appreciation of the Catholic Faith in general or of the power of the grace of the Sacrament of Marriage in particular. Every one of them could be remedied if scandal did not keep that supernatural appreciation dumb!

And please do not think that I know nothing of the pressures that can defeat what I am saying. I was married for thirty years to a Catholic uncanonized saint. For eighteen years of that time I was a belligerent Protestant but she taught me the supernatural appreciation of the Bond of Marriage and the power of Sacramental Grace to meet every situation which can arise.

And by the same token, the supernatural grace of the Sacrament of Marriage can serve to make a team out of the whole family, each working for all, across any age-gap that can exist. It is indeed true that the snowball of scandal exerts increasing pressures on young and old in these days but the exercise of supernatural faith and grace will find the answer for those who trust God, *come what may,* and pray to Him constantly and use the Sacraments which God provides in the Church.

All this is especially true as regards vocations to the priesthood and the Religious Life. I recently received a clipping from a secular newspaper sent to me by a Catholic layman in considerable distress. The clipping voiced the sentiments of the head of a large seminary in the United States. The tenor of it was to urge seminaries to cultivate personal initiative to stimulate vocations. But in his zeal to urge his point he voiced a sentiment which has definitely become a part of the snowball of scandal. He voiced the opinion that a twelve year course of seminary training starting with high school, amounts to brainwashing.

What could be more skillfully devised to daunt the budding spark of a vocation in the heart of a high school boy or his parents? Furthermore, this advice is directly contrary to the teaching of all of our popes of the past hundred years.

It is precisely in these days of worldly pressure that boys need to be strengthened by the supernatural environment of a seminary. They must be helped to resist the ever-growing pressures that minimize the colossal privilege that God offers to make one His special instrument for the salvation of souls. The only valid incentive to the priesthood or the religious life is a supernatural one. This cannot be expected to emerge except in the supernatural atmosphere of the family of deep faith. It cannot be sustained without the supernatural atmosphere of the Catholic Seminary.

God keeps all that *is* in being from moment to moment and offers us evidence of His own choosing to invite us to trust Him. In fact, it seems that the whole purpose of this universe and us in it, is to classify souls who will take this evidence that God provides and let Him make us suitable for His eternal love.

This lends itself to the somewhat terrifying conclusion that God permits the Devil to function because he is the world's most expert classifier of souls. God demands our love but as a guarantee of the *nature* of our love, He demands our *trust*. Trust is, of course, an aspect of faith but it is the aspect that we can give that makes us eligible for the Gift from God of the supernatural Grace of Faith. And that is all that we need to make us utterly secure against the turmoil of the Modern World and the Modern Church.

There is an excellent book published in 1968, entitled: *Keeping Your Balance in the Modern Church* by the Redemptorist Father Hugh J. O'Connell. His thesis is that the confusion in today's theology is the result of failure to distinguish the relationship between God's objective revelation and the inner religious experience in the consciousness of the individual man. The whole book develops the answer and it is well worth reading for every Catholic. But when all is said and done there is one very simple answer that covers all the rest. It is this: Our Faith is a supernatural gift from God. It is guaranteed for us by God and is made known to us in every age by the Teaching Authority which God has provided and protects from error.

Father O'Connell expresses this very hopefully. After showing the defects in the welter of theological discussion going on today, he continues: "At this point the average Catholic may be tempted to throw up his hands and cry out: 'How am I to discover the truth in the religious controversies swirling around me? If even some Catholic theologians, priests and nuns are getting off the track, how am I to find the way to the truth?'

"The Answer", Father O'Connell says, "is very simple and very clear: Listen to the Teaching Authority of the Church! And this means, to the Pope and to the College of Bishops. They alone are the official teachers of the Church. . . ." It is quite clear from the multitude of religious opinions around us today, that the infallible guidance of the Holy Spirit, which Christ promised to His Church, is *not* found outside of this Teaching Authority.

You will note that I have not quoted a word of Scripture in support of my assertions. That is because my thesis starts where proof leaves off. It does not mean that the proof is not there. But the truth of what I have told you should be an incentive for anyone who feels the slightest anxiety in the present situation, to do what it takes to whet his trust in God by making a fresh survey of the evidence. But before you start I would like to give you the perspective expressed in Psalm 88 a thousand years before Jesus Christ gave the evidence that *God's Reign is Perfect:*

> O Lord God of hosts, who is your equal?
> You are mighty, O Lord, and truth is your garment.
> It is you who rule the sea in its pride;
> it is you who still the surging of its waves.
> The heavens are yours, the world is yours.
> It is you who founded the earth and all it holds;

it is you who created the North and the South.
Tabor and Hermon shout with joy at your name.
Yours is a mighty arm, O Lord;
your hand is strong, your right hand ready.
Justice and right are the pillars of your throne,
love and truth walk in your presence.
Happy the people who acclaim such a king,
who walk, O Lord, in the light of your face,
who find their joy every day in your name.
who make your justice the source of their bliss.

Ps. 88:9–17

Equipped with this conviction, every faithful Catholic may know that, in obedience to Christ's Vicar, our Holy Father, he will find unity, security, and the certainty of doing God's will.

Some time ago I had an experience which crystallized in my mind our grave need to ask ourselves the question which forms the title of this chapter, *What are we here for?* and to remind us of the scandal of dissent that makes that question needed. I was asked to lead the Rosary before the funeral of a beautiful little twelve-year-old daughter of a large Catholic family. This was before the English wording of the creeds had been changed and as I opened the recitation of the Apostles Creed, there were perhaps twenty friends and relatives who knelt in the little chapel. When I concluded my part with the clause, "From thence He shall come to judge the living and the dead," there followed a prodigious silence which surprised me so that it was several seconds before I could carry on with that final sentence of infinite promise: "I believe in the Holy Spirit; the Holy Catholic Church; the Communion of Saints; the forgiveness of sins; the Resurrection of the body and the life everlasting."

Now, I do not mean to imply that this silence represented a denial of the very essence of Catholic

Faith. It is, however, indicative of a state of mind which is vulnerable to grave injury and scandal as a result of the many detestable denials of the faith which are thoughtlessly or maliciously being broadcast today. God has offered the people of the world an absolute and infallible guarantee of adequate guidance. He has provided, first and foremost, a Teaching Authority to which He has guaranteed the constant guidance of His Holy Spirit to enable each and every one of us to know His will and all of the priceless treasury of faith which He has revealed. He has provided us with His Holy Catholic Church and its saving Sacrifice of Mass, its Sacraments and its Holy Father who is fortified to keep our faith awake and vivid by his guidance.

Throughout the life of this Church, however, there have been times when the "Gates of Hell", as Christ called the forces opposed to His Church, have taken advantage of current events to attack and molest the Church and to tempt believers to fall away.

God in His infinite wisdom, allows this to happen as a discipline to weed out those who are so apathetic toward their Faith that they do not even know its esesence in the Apostles Creed.

The present day is definitely one of the times when the Church is besieged by the Gates of Hell. It has indeed been worse in times past, but never have there been so many members of the Church Militant who have spinelessly or maliciously made themselves vulnerable to the daunting of the Devil by allowing their faith to be attacked by a disobedient minority.

The Devil has been frantically encouraging this disobedience. It has taken chiefly the form of dissent from some of the essential elements of our faith. Instead of being daunted by the extent of this attack, it is a grave duty of every one of us to stand up and be counted as an active supporter of the faith as it is defended for us by our Holy Father.

His Eminence, Jean Cardinal Danielou, in his splendid book entitled *The Faith Eternal and the Man of Today,* has this to say: "The Faith is not a reality which we have a right to change as we please. It is our absolute duty to protest against any alteration of that to which we have rightly committed our life." And he continues, "This does not in the least mean that the Christian attitude is a fixed, set, ultra-conservative attitude. The datum of faith is immutable in its content but our understanding of it is something that can grow indefinitely. . . . And, therein lies the prodigious adventure of the Christian intellect, of constantly striving to reach an even greater understanding of what was given once and for all. . . . But today we have another conception of the intellect, which sees it not as plumbing reality but as contesting it."

And that has been the masterpiece of the Devil in these post-conciliar years. The behavior of all too many priests and bishops in opposition to our God-given means of understanding our faith, has poisoned the minds of countless souls whose faith has never had a supernatural anchor in the promises of Christ. This constitutes a threat to the very existence of the Church as we have known it.

This sort of attack has been directed against many items of our faith, but one of the most deadly features of it has been the avalanche of dissent against the perennial teaching of the Catholic Church expressed in the Encyclical Letter "Humanae Vitae" of our beloved Holy Father of happy memory, Pope Paul VI. The evil of this attack is emphasized when we realize that "Humanae Vitae" does not even suggest any modification in what has always been the infallible declaration of God's law as taught by the Church.

This is *the* outstanding example of the diabolical misuse of the cliche "It's not infallible." It is true that encyclical letters are not declared as "Ex Cathedra" but the fact remains that there is nothing in the Encyclical "Humanae Vitae" which departs from what has always been the perennial teaching of the Catholic Church expounding the law of God. To violate this law or to advise others that it is not binding in conscience is to make one's self guilty of grave sin.

The Encyclical sets forth, perhaps in clearer terms than ever before, that any direct form of artificial limitation of the natural process of procreation is objectively sinful.

What could be more definite than these words of the Encyclical? "Each and every marriage act must remain open to the transmission of life. . . . The direct interruption of the generative process already begun, and above all, directly willed and procured abortion, even for therapeutic reasons, is to be absolutely excluded as licit means of regulating birth. Equally excluded, as the Teaching Authority of the Church has frequently declared, is direct sterilization, whether perpetual or temporary, whether of the man or of the woman. Similarly excluded is every action which, either in anticipation of the conjugal act, or in its accomplishment, or in the development of its natural consequences, purposes, whether as an end or as a means, to render procreation impossible."

All this is presented in a form which has always been recognized as a part of the "ordinary" infallible teaching of the Church pertaining to the law which binds all men and women of the world as ordained by God. If the Holy Father had attempted to change it, God would have intervened to prevent the denial of His law and the consequent collapse of His Holy

Catholic Church. How can it be that the deniers are so blind?

Nevertheless, it has been maintained in various media of communication available to hundreds of millions of people, that one who, in his conscience does not agree with this teaching, is free to disregard it without guilt of sin. Not only is this a detestable denial of the law of God and of the Catholic Faith, but it is a scandal that is wrecking the lives of millions of souls. Of the propagators of scandal, Christ has said: It were better for them if a mill-stone were hung about their necks and they were cast into the sea!

The sin of contraception may be forgiven if it is confessed with true contrition and honest purpose of amendment, but disagreement with the law of God will never lessen the gravity of the sin. It has long since ceased to be a purely personal matter. It has assumed the form of an attack against the very existence of the Church and it is of vital importance to each and every one of us *now!*

CHAPTER III

A NEW PENTECOST IN THE SOULS OF MEN

Our beloved Holy Father of happy memory, Pope John XXIII, frequently referred to the Second Vatican Council as the source of *a new Pentecost in the souls of men*. The idea behind this vision of Pope John is different from the *old Pentecost* which we celebrate each year fifty days after Easter. The indwelling of the Holy Spirit is the precious privilege of every Christian who perseveres in a state of Sanctifying Grace. It should be cherished with humility and made evident by a life of adoring love and calm serenity in the face of the noisy pressure of Atheism which has killed the true *supernatural* nature of the faith of all too many believers. It is an exhibition of presumptuous pride to boast of it!

The ultimate success of the purpose for which Pope John called the Second Vatican Council, depends upon one thing only: A change within the souls of men and women and children throughout the world. The change desired is the awakening or the strengthening of true *supernatural* faith in the following words and promises addressed by Jesus Christ to Saint Peter and the other Apostles:

"Thou art Peter and upon this rock I will build My Church and the Gates of Hell shall not prevail against it." (Matt. 16:18).

"All power in Heaven and on earth hath been given to Me. Go ye therefore, make disciples of all nations, baptizing them in the name of the Father and of the Son and of the Holy Spirit: teaching them to observe all that I have commanded you: and behold, I am with you all days unto the consummation of the world." (Matt. 28:18-20).

"And the Advocate, the Holy Spirit, whom the Father will send in My Name, He shall teach you all things, and bring to your mind all the things that I have said to you." (John 14:26).

"And when He shall have come, the Spirit of Truth, He shall guide you to the whole truth." (John 16:13).

And finally: "He that heareth you heareth Me; and he that rejecteth you rejecteth Me: and he that rejecteth Me rejecteth Him who sent Me." (Luke 10:16).

Jesus summed up all these words in the prayer which He addressed to the Father on the eve of His Passion which sealed His bond with men: "Hallow them in the truth; Thy word is the Truth. As Thou didst send Me into the world: so I sent them into the world; and for their sake I consecrate Myself, that they also may be consecrated in truth. But I ask not only for them, but also for those who believe in Me through their word, that they all may be one; that, as Thou, Father, art in Me, and I am in Thee, they also may be one in Us."(Jn. 17:17-21).

All of these words taken together form an important part of the motive for our faith and the conviction that all of it is taught by God and guaranteed by Him to be protected from error. The intrinsic truth of each item of the deposit of truth may be acceptable to our human reason, but the only Catholic motive for believing it is that it is told to us by God. All this is the *motive* for faith. Faith itself, however, is a purely supernatural act of the will when it is moved by the grace of God to accept the deposit of faith as guaranteed by Him and made known here and now by the Infallible Teaching Authority chosen by Him. It is impossible to over-emphasize this concept of faith and every Catholic soul should be reminded of it frequently in these days when the exploitation of science is confusing so many half-instructed souls.

Faith is not a perfect and static act of the will which, once made, is valid for life, as taught by some Protestant sects. On the contrary, it is a supernatural virtue which can be possessed in any degree from a very fragile beginning to a certainty bordering almost on vision which was the prerogative of the Blessed Virgin Mary. Faith can be cultivated and strengthened by cooperation with grace and it can be lost altogether by resistance to grace.

But the possession of supernatural faith is only the first step toward sanctification. It is, indeed, a necessary first step toward the infinitely greater and more precious treasure of Sanctifying Grace which supernaturalizes the soul in the Sacrament of Baptism or which brings a supernaturally dead soul back to life in the Sacrament of Penance. It is really and truly an infinite treasure because—impossible yet true—the Triune God takes up His abode within the soul and remains there all life long unless He is driven out by the perfidy of mortal sin. So, when all is said and done, the sole purpose of Christ's sojourn upon earth and the founding of His Church has been to give glory to God by drawing all men into the company of the elect by that indwelling presence of God in sanctifying grace in every soul.

The essential work of the Church, then, is supernatural and spiritual and, therefore, invisible because it takes place in the souls of men. That, however, does not mean that its effect cannot be very plainly seen by all men because, by the wisdom of God, the bodies of men are so intimately united with their souls that the indwelling presence of God may be said to permeate the whole personality, body and soul, and reflect in all that each one does as a child of God.

In exactly the same way the true ministration of the Church to its members is all spiritual. First, it leads them to spiritual re-birth as temples of the Holy Spirit in Baptism. Then it builds up the supernatural treasures as Saint Peter reminds us in his Epistle: "Employ all care to furnish your faith with virtue, your virtue with knowledge, your knowledge with self-control, your self-control with patience, your patience with piety, your piety with brotherly love, brotherly love with charity. For if these things exist and increase in you, they will make you neither idle nor unfruitful in the full knowledge of our Lord Jesus Christ." (II Peter 1:5-8). And all this is fortified by the channels of grace abiding in the Sacrifice of Mass and the Sacraments and sacramentals and, finally and always, by that ever precious Infallible Teaching Authority, guiding us in prayer.

Let us sum up, then, the objective of the *new Pentecost* in just two sentences: The first sentence is this: God, in His wisdom, demands that man, in order to keep and strengthen and really *own* this treasure of Sanctifying Grace, must use his will all life long, as it were to *earn* it. The second sentence is this: Of course a finite creature could not possibly really earn the possession of the infinite God in his soul, but God, in His infinite love, has provided that the purpose of man's life in this world shall be to truly earn the preservation and adornment of this infinite gift, in partnership with God, by meeting and repelling all the invitations of the Devil and his angels, which we know as temptations, to disobey or neglect the rules which God has attached to man's possession of God in Sanctifying Grace. These last two sentences really state the meaning of our life in this world and give the reason why God allows the Devil to interfere with our spiritual wellbeing.

A New Pentecost in the Souls of Men

We may seem to spend all our time doing a great variety of things which have no relations to those two sentences. We may seem to be earning a living, winning fame, using the world's goods, begetting children, defending ourselves against aggression, giving indispensable services to our neighbors—all this is merely the setting in which God watches us train our wills to be the kind of people God wants around Himself in heaven! That is the only work that counts with God. The rest is merely incidental. The souls of each and every human being in this world at this moment, one might say, are the only precious part of creation in God's eyes. The harvest of souls, each possessing the seed of glory by God's indwelling presence, is the true work for which God has made the world—and man.

All this sounds so simple and so obvious that it might seem to the new arrival from Mars that it would be inconceivable that the Devil would get any hearing at all. But the weary Catholic wayfarer would explain that, strange as it may seem, there are two apparent flaws in the scheme which account for the paradox of many souls who seem to be satisfied with the husks that feed swine instead of the possession of God. First, there is the crippled condition of the mind and will which man has inherited from our first parents. This makes it possible for him to allow the present attraction of the husks which he can see and handle, to dim his understanding of the truth which God insists he must accept with only God's word for guarantee, and which God always leaves him free to refuse. Second, there is the appalling cunning of the Devil who has never ceased to take full advantage of that victory he did win over the free-will of our first parents. Indeed, man would be no match for the Devil were it not for the fact that all his activity is minutely under the control of almighty God who permits his diabolical deception only to an extent sufficient to exercise and prove souls worthy to be candidates for heaven.

And there is the really awesome crux of the whole situation. God is so jealous of the quality of loving trust which He insists upon for the souls who are going to live with Him for all eternity, that He will not ever coerce a soul that resists His grace. This does not mean that, to be a candidate for heaven man must raise *himself* to that caliber of love. That was the error of Pelagius so violently condemned by Saint Augustine. It would also savor of the Jansenism which wrecked the faith of many in France in the seventeenth century. No! the testing which God permits is to prove those with enough humility to distrust themselves and to trust with submissive love in the sufficiency of God's grace at all times. "Blessed is the man who endures temptation for when he is proved he will receive the crown of life which God has promised to them that love Him" (James 1:2).

It is always pride that makes one vulnerable to the wiles of Satan, for God resists the proud and gives His loving help of grace to the humble. Somehow that blight on our wills bequeathed upon us by Adam seems to breed in us that same urge of pride that that makes it seem belittling to be so utterly dependent upon God. At least that is the only way to account for the number of men who allow the temptation to disobey God to cause them to rebel, to turn and, in effect, to spit in Christ's face and say with Lucifer, "Non serviam"—"I will not submit." And yet, these are the very ones Christ wants to save from themselves: " I came not to call the just, but sinners to repentance." (Matt. 9:13).

That does not mean that God is not interested in those in whose hearts He is living even now. Quite the contrary, Christ's own humility makes Him say that He, almighty God, *needs* our help to win the rest. Indeed, there is one sense in which God *does* actually need our help to win souls under the rules that He, Himself has laid down. He has provided us, in His goodness, with an Infallible Teaching Authority, but He leaves us utterly free to cooperate with grace and believe its teaching or to go our own sweet way and reject grace and refuse belief. An infallible Teaching Authority is of no avail unless some of us believe.

Suppose for a moment the impossible; suppose that suddenly every lay person in the world should deny his faith and thrust God out of his soul. The Magisterium could plead until doomsday, but no one would believe. The world would, in very truth, be raising hell. The hands of Christ would indeed be nailed to the Cross in vain. The Church-Teaching is nothing without the Church-Believing. Christ does need the example of each one of us who will believe and who will try to keep Him dwelling in his heart. He needs us because He has willed to need us, not because He lacks the power to guide this world as He has planned it.

And that is what is meant by the *Communion of Saints*. Each one who believes has important work to do for those who are now in the world and for those who are still to come into it, as well as for those in Purgatory. And that is what I have been leading up to in all that I have said thus far. Perhaps you sometimes think: " What incentive is there for me to do more than merely to try to keep God in my soul and remain in a state of grace?" It is the answer to that question that is the purpose of this chapter.

I have said that God in His Providence has disposed the running of the world so that He needs our prayers and our good works, but His reason for needing them is because He loves us so much that He wishes, of His bounty, to reward our help a thousand-fold more than it is worth! In other words, the true incentive for goodness is such that if faith were vision we would all be saints. It is the depth of the *Supernatural* Faith of each one of us that tells us how much God needs us and gives us the urge to do our part. The perfect victory would bring God into every soul in the world, in sanctifying grace. Failure to reach that perfect victory will not mean that God's power is less than infinite, but that He insists that each individual victory hinges upon an individual choice of the will aided by His grace and by the work of the Communion of Saints. Each one of us is an important member of that Communion of Saints!

I have compared the Prelates who were assembled at Rome to the officers of the Church militant, the officers of the Kingdom of Truth, of Justice, of Love, and of Peace—to use the words of the prayer of Pope John XXIII. The Church is not militant *against* souls, but is militant *for* souls, against the ideas of deceitfulness in place of truth, of license in place of justice, of lust in place of love, and of persecution in place of peace. These evil ideas become lodged in the souls of men by reason of their cooperation with the Devil and his angels. Such men then become, themselves, the agents of the Devil. And, exactly because the tools of the Devil are not restricted by justice, love and truth, they become the agents of lying, treacherous, deceitful propaganda bent on burying the teaching of truth beneath a smear of doubt and hate. And because of the sheer bulk of this lying propaganda, many souls, even of men of good-will, are led away from the truth so that it comes about that they are unwitting agents of Satan who, as Christ warned, will "think they do God service by putting you to death." (John 16:2).

Such was the lying propaganda which the Devil used in the eleventh and sixteenth centuries to tear Christendom asunder and such is the atmosphere which we have inherited today which prompts missionaries of Satan, who have been reared from childhood to abhor the Catholic Church, to go into foreign lands and suffer all sorts of hardships to fight in opposition to the Catholic Church and the message given to her by Christ. In this present day the Devil has more clients than ever before in the history of the world. There are many reasons for this. The most obvious one is, of course, the tremendous recent increase in the population of the world. But the most poisonous reason is the acceptance of the hint insinuated by the Devil into the proud hearts of many students of natural science that their findings have made man the master of the material world and in so doing have made a myth of God and the supernatural.

These were two important reasons for the calling of the Second Vatican Council. But the calling of the Council itself stirred the Devil into a frenzy of rage that has goaded the agents of Atheism all over the world. They have increased their pace because they realize, as very few Catholics do, what it would do to their cause if all of Christendom were really united into the one Kingdom of the Divine Savior. God has allowed this to come about to convince us of our need for Him and His need for us to do our part and to show us the momentous importance of these post-conciliar years and the importance of the responsibility of each and every Christian.

How complete would be the change all over the world if *all* of Christendom became united in one *supernatural* union of souls bent on bringing to all the world the *same* message from Christ. Atheism would have little to offer in opposition to a Christendom united in *Supernatural Faith*. But without union it is we who have little proof of the infinite treasure we have to offer.

Let us think with a little more detail of just what our part involves. First and foremost, we must realize that God needs us only because He has chosen to make us instruments of His power. It is the people of the Catholic Church seen one by one and all in one, who offer the most potent invitation to the rest of the world to join them. The Devil is hacking at these people one by one and all in one, to help them to botch that invitation. He is also hacking away at those who are being invited, to help them to hear the lies and to be aware of the scandals that will keep them from learning the truth.

This combination has, to some extent, caused the appeal of the Church to become obscured in this twentieth century and that is one of the reasons why our late Holy Father called the Second Vatican Council. Its first purpose was to remove all the obstacles from within which had weakened the solid front of the faithful. It was to overhaul the discipline, clarify the doctrine, perfect the teaching methods, amplify the availability of the Sacraments and the Sacrifice of Mass, and unify the administration of government. The manifold misinterpretations of the Documents of the Council have, however, hatefully interfered with the success of this objective. The final effect and success of it all will depend upon two great power-plants of grace, that mysterious force that God uses to fortify the hearts of men.

The first power-plant is the post-conciliar organization of the Church working directly at the outlet of that great ocean of grace which is furnished by the Holy Spirit. The second power-plant is in the heart of you and me and five hundred million other yous and mes all over the world, responding to the grace from the Council and reflecting it upon every

A New Pentecost in the Souls of Men 33

man, woman, and child in the world. If you and I cooperate and use and reflect the grace that is available, we shall all become saints. To the extent that we do become saints, God will use that power to snatch souls from the Devil, one by one and all in one, until we will begin to see the triumph of the Kingdom of the Divine Savior; the Kingdom of Truth, of Justice, of Love, and of Peace.

We will probably not all become saints, but that will not be God's fault. He is furnishing us the power and the incentive and will do most of the work. Success will be measured by the collective sum-total of our individual response to the call to each of us to *initiate a new Pentecost in the souls of men,* starting today! The material will be perfect faith, the incentive God-within-us. We can begin by bringing to our minds, day by day and many times every day, our own individual *Project Sainthood.* Do this, not only to achieve your own sanctification, but to contribute to a colossal example to others to pursue the same course!

We can each start on a small scale or in a more energetic way. The important thing is to allow project sainthood to color everything we do, as if each thing we do and say were being watched by others who are learning from our example. Each thing we do is more effective than we realize, especially when God is standing by to make it count. Every little prayer, every little ejaculation, every checking of the tongue from an impulse to a tart remark, every thoughtful act of charity for the benefit of others, every sacrifice made to do the corporal works of mercy, every sacrifice you make in order to be present at weekday Mass and Communion, every recitation of the Rosary, every thoughtful spiritual Communion made during any day. You may not start them all at once, but if you will let project sainthood become an integral part of your life, you will soon begin to experience the joy of helping to create *A New Pentecost in the Souls of Men.*

CHAPTER IV
DAILY MASS: THE SOURCE OF POWER

Let us now consider in some detail our individual sharing in the output of the two power-plants of supernatural witness provided by the Catholic Church to invite all men by our example to a *new Pentecost*.

It was mentioned that the Sacraments and the Sacrifice of Mass are the most prominent visible signs of the functioning of these power-houses. It is our individual privilege and obligation to make the invisible output of these power-houses apparent to the outside world of men. This we do, or fail to do, by our example of zeal for our faith or by our neglect of it and our example of scandal which is all the more avidly broadcast to the world by haters of the Church.

Those who wish to be *Menders of the Mess* that now prevails can best fortify their souls for action by constant union with Christ stemming from the Sacrifice of Mass. The welcoming words of Christ invite each one of us to share in this source of power: "Come you blessed of My Father! Inherit the Kingdom prepared for you from the foundation of the world." (Matt. 25-34).

A recent magazine article entitled "Modern Antiques" mentioned a number of things that have become museum pieces that are anxiously sought after by the property-men of T.V. and motion picture producers. Among the things mentioned was the old-fashioned alarm-clock with a bell attached at the top. They have become obsolete because they were not very dependable and had to be wound up every day and frequently checked to keep them running accurately.

These clocks have been replaced because the great network of intercommunicating power-houses throughout the land has made synchronized electric power so dependable that clocks driven by it will often run for many months, or even years, without noticeable variation in time. The reason for this is that central stations are kept in touch with the observatory source of astronomical time correction.

By means of this improvement in the ordering of our work and sleep we are able to use our time to better advantage and to arrange our temporal affairs with greater confidence and do better work for ourselves and for each other. All of the improvements in the tools of our temporal affairs which modern science and mechanical invention have given to us have made it possible for us to enjoy much more fruitful use of God's natural gifts to us. It is quite certain that God is pleased that we should enjoy these increased blessings of His gifts.

On the other hand, it might be well for us to ask ourselves just how this added joy is pleasing to God. We already know at least part of the answer. All of our use of our natural blessings is pleasing to God because, and to the extent that, we see in it the proof of God's goodness and power and love and we are drawn thereby to love God more and to be grateful to Him. In other words, the riches of nature are given to us by God to bring us closer to an appreciation of the infinitely more precious riches of our supernatural relationship to God.

All too often, however, Catholics who are less sensitive in their appreciation of values than those I have called *Menders of the Mess*, allow the enjoyment of worldly goods and natural delights to obscure for them the good that God offers us in the supernatural world rather than to heighten their appreciation of it. In order to guard ourselves against

Daily Mass—The Source of Power 37

the slightest danger of this contamination we should try to find the reason for it and, having found the reason, we should try to turn it to our advantage. If we succeed we will not only turn it to our advantage, but we will know far better how to make it understood by those spiritually and materially less fortunate people who are the beneficiaries of the work of *menders*.

The first and most obvious reason is that our five natural senses are precisely designed to permit us to appreciate and enjoy the natural world. Furthermore, these natural senses do not give us any direct access to the supernatural world. Our access to the latter stems from those properties of man's soul which God referred to when He said: "Let us make man in our own image and likeness." (Gen. 1:26). That is the power to know, to will, and to love. Unfortunately, however, these powers have been blighted by Original Sin so that they do not easily exercise their proper dominion even when the seed of supernatural life is restored by Baptism. Thus we see that we are fully equipped to enter into and enjoy all the treasures of the natural world and are inclined by our appetites to place them first in our desires. Our equipment, on the other hand, to appraise and enter into the enjoyment of the supernatural world is lacking in that perception which corresponds to sight and hearing, etc. It is blunted even as to those indirect faculties which should lead us in the right direction.

On the face of it, it looks as if the odds are quite definitely against our choosing the joys that are hidden in God in preference to those which we can grasp so easily as they surround us. And that "on-the-face-of-it" answer is what explains completely the present plight of the world of men who seem to be poised on the brink of self-extermination. Reason alone can tell us that this world we see and the men in it simply could not be here unless it were in the complete control of the almighty Creator of it all. But one look at the world makes it fairly plain that reason, going it alone, has made a very sorry mess of utilizing even the material treasures that God has given us.

Fortunately, however, God has not left the matter entirely to reason alone. He has given us the certainty of Revelation made in a way that reason would never have dreamed of because it betrays a love for man which is so far beyond anything that man is able to return that reason cannot easily bridge the gap. God's love for His ungrateful creature, man, as shown by every step of the whole story of His Incarnation, together with its sacramental continuation to the present day, is so prodigious as to be, when judged by human standards, absolutely unbelievable!

And there is the answer to the whole unanswerable status of the world today: God does not ask us to judge by human standards, He asks us to *believe* —to believe in spite of the "impossibleness" of God-made-Man; to believe in spite of the "impossibleness" of God-dying-on-the-Cross; to believe in spite of the "impossibleness" of God bringing His Sacrifice of the Cross onto our altars here and now, all day, every day.

The somewhat terrifying aspect of the whole thing is that God *asks* our belief on the strength of His word alone. He does not *demand* belief. Nowhere in revelation are we told: "Thou shalt believe!" Saint John's Gospel and Epistles are filled with exhortations to believe, but never is it commanded. "Blessed are they," Christ said to Saint Thomas, "who have not seen and yet believe" (John 20:29). The spiritual chaos in the world today gives every evidence of the failure of most men to heed Christ's invitation and promises.

The world is, however, as God intends it to be, a vale of tears, to temper our free-will into love. God hates sin and He hates unbelief, but He is so jealous of your free-will and mine that He will let the whole world fall apart if need be, rather than comply with the demand of the high priest that He come down from the Cross and compel those who do not will to believe. He gives the grace to believe and, as Saint Thomas Aquinas tells us, He moves the will to believe, but by His mysterious power, the will must move freely to cooperate with grace.

So—faith is a gift from God, but it is a gift that can be refused. And so it is with the fruits of grace every step of the way through life. It is not just the beginning of grace that requires the unconditional surrender of our free-will. It is the day by day acceptance of the Cross for no other reason than that Christ has said: "If any man has a mind to come My way, let him renounce self, and take up his cross and follow Me." (Matt 16:24).

To the average Catholic lay person it sometimes seems hard that the choice of the Cross should be so repugnant as compared with the easy way offered by the world. But those who have been invited by Christ to become His *menders* have been given the grace to see that Christ intended that it should be so. In fact, the more one enters into Christ's plan, the more he learns that it is by accepting the difficult crosses that one can not only show his love for Christ, but can actually build up that love and the Sanctifying Grace that goes with it.

That is what makes those who enter fully into it, the most likely candidates for sainthood to be found among the workers in Christ's vineyard. Instead of being daunted by the terror of the Cross, you know that Christ chose it because, as He said, "it was necessary for Him to have suffered those things, and so to enter into His glory." (Luke 24:26). The reasón that it was necesary was to show our dull imagination the infinite malice of sin, the infinite love of God, and the infinite incentive for us to love Him and to enter into His glory with him by taking up the crosses He offers us.

It is to keep us mindful of this incentive for the Cross that the Church lays such great emphasis on the power of prayer and the effectiveness of prayer as a great part of the works of charity which you and I are invited to perform. And that is why I opened this chapter with the little story about the clocks that keep the temporal world functioning in an efficient manner because they are all connected to a vast network of power plants all synchronized by observatory time.

The Catholic Church today is really just that in the spiritual world. It is a world-wide network of power plants using the pressure of prayer to generate grace and distribute it to souls all over the world. Our altars are the generators. They are activated by the Sacrifice of Mass generating power day and night throughout the world all synchronized to the heart-beat of the Sun of Justice benignly ordering all things sweetly from His heavenly throne.

I do not wish to push the analogy too far, but one might easily imagine the monasteries and convents, especially those of cloistered religious, as substations transforming the fervent prayer of the Mass into the domestic channels of grace; and every priest and religious reciting the Divine Office privately as individual auxiliary transformers. Through our beloved Mother, too, we children of Mary may be very special accessory instruments, used more directly by Christ's Mother who is the Mistress of all the plants. You may be chosen to operate under her

Daily Mass—The Source of Power 41

special attention if you keep yourself close to the source of all this power by your attachment to her.

And now to give the analogy one last little pat: you can most effectively become a part of the colossal example referred to in the previous chapter if you keep yourself in mesh with the heart-beat of Christ by that daily orientation furnished by daily Mass and Communion. This will keep you in mesh all day, every day, and make you a very special instrument of Christ just as priests and religious are very special instruments of Christ as purveyors of grace to others and examples to invite them also to daily Mass and Communion and weekly confession.

Sometimes missionaries and retreat-masters, when talking among themselves, will argue that it is not prudent to urge too strongly the merit of daily Mass and Communion for fear of discouraging those who think it would be impossible for them. I am sure, however, that there is no such danger in speaking to those whom Christ invites to be *menders*. You have zeal and courage or you would not be thinking of Christ. You also know that the success of your every task is dependent, not on your skill or dexterity, but rather upon your direct connection with Christ.

It is your bodily presence at the Sacrifice of Mass and the real Presence of the Body and Blood of Christ in Communion that will make you His perfect instrument because then you will be in perfect mesh with the heart-beat of Christ in doing His will on earth as it is in heaven. It is the infallible bond of love which dispels every vestige of obscurity which stands between the natural and the supernatural and places you on the surest route to sanctification which can be found on this earth.

I ask forgiveness if I repeat here a part of the story of my own introduction to daily Mass and

Communion as told at length in my life-story. When I was a small boy my father was a devout Low Church Episcopalian. He taught me to love and to look forward to the weekly Communion Service which was as near as it could be to an English translation of the Roman Canon of the Mass. When I first attended a Catholic Mass I did not recognize the slightest connection and it meant nothing whatever to me. But when I finally did understand it and was received into the Catholic Church, I was so delighted that I learned by heart all the Latin of the Common of the Mass, from beginning to end. Little did I realize then, in what good stead it would stand me eighteen years later when I had to learn to offer the Mass myself as a priest. But at the start it made me love the Mass because I could understand what it all meant and could watch the priest instead of scrambling through the book. Now, of course, the Mass in the vernacular offers every one that same joy.

It was five years after that that my wife and I attended during Lent, what was called a "Rosary Novena" given by a dear old Paulist Father. It involved attending daily Mass and Communion together with a Rosary and an instruction for twenty-seven consecutive days. Toward the end of the time the Father began discreetly to suggest the blessings of continuing the practice of daily Mass and Communion although he was quite aware of the difficulty involved for many people leading busy lives in the world.

The first morning after the close of the "Novena" I told my wife that I was making no promises, but I was going to try out the Father's suggestion from day to day. I also said that I did not want her to go, just to please me—but she went with me. Neither of us ever made any promise or pledge, but we very

Daily Mass—The Source of Power 43

soon discovered that, while breakfast might be missed if necessary, we would never miss Mass—and we never did—until the day of her death seven years later, except for the time she spent in the hopsital, and even then she received daily Communion.

That was more than forty years ago so I can tell you from experience that when Christ promised one-hundredfold reward to those who would give up worldly delights for His sake—He was not addressing those only who would enter the priesthood or religious life, but to all who will make any sacrifices for His sake—He keeps His promise. So, even if it is truly impossible for you to reap the one-hundredfold reward of daily Mass and Communion and the richness which it would add to all your work, you may go at least sometimes, and may always reap the benefit of weekly Confession and weekly Communion.

Furthermore, you may be assured that any and all of the work and prayer that you undertake for Christ is definitely included among the sacrifices for His sake which Christ had in mind when He said: "There is no one who has forsaken home, or brothers, or sisters, or mother, or father, or children, or lands, for My sake and the Gospel's, but shall receive a hundred times as much now, in the present time—houses, brothers, sisters, mothers, children, and lands, together with persecutions—and, in the world to come, life everlasting." (Mark 10:29).

It is not these things alone for which Christ promised the reward, but all detachment from the things the world seeks, when done for His sake and for the sake of the Gospel. And that, even though one is persecuted for doing them. The things you do as *menders* are, you may be sure, very dear to Christ and the more you can enrich them by meshing your life with the prayer and Sacrifice of the Church and tying yourself to Christ by Holy Communion, the greater will be your reward and the greater your joy in doing it now, and the greater your assurance of hearing those final words of Christ: "Come, you blessed of My Father! Inherit the Kingdom prepared for you from the foundation of the world. . . . Indeed, I tell you, as long as you did these things to one of the least of these My brethren, you did so to Me." (Matt. 25:34 & 40).

The present state of the world, as reported day after day in the news, makes it obvious that unless a very much larger percentage of Christian people turn to Christ in this way, *there is grave danger ahead!*

CHAPTER V

GOD'S LAW AND MAN'S LAW

Saint Peter has given us a formula for loyal Catholic *Menders of the Mess* to use to meet the *danger* of Supernatural Blindness that is besetting the world, when he says: "For this is the will of God: that you should silence by your good conduct the ignorance of foolish men." (I. Peter 2:15).

It would be hard to find a good Catholic in North America who does not have some relationship with non-Catholics of sufficient intimacy to make one's influence and example a matter of profound importance to both. A Catholic's way of life is a direct reflection of his depth of Faith. His action and attitude and ideas stem from the motives which his Faith inspires. Every Catholic has, therefore, a grave responsibility to examine his Faith and his conformity to the will of God so that his example *will* silence the ignorance of foolish men.

The opposite example in this regard is the pitiful failure of millions of Catholics who do not heed the will of God in their attitude toward contraception and sinful sexual behavior. The huge bulk of this sinful example is probably the greatest *danger* to supernatural Faith existing in the world today. It is the source of the attitude that prompts most of the disloyalty to the Holy See and hence the decay of Faith. So let us seek to clinch our Faith in a way that will help us to know and follow God's Law rather than Man's Law.

The most aggravated form of the need for good example on the part of Catholics is, of course, found in mixed-marriage because it is the most intimate relationship possible between two human beings and also because it is the relationship most intimately involving that most mooted moral issue—unnatural birth-prevention.

The same difficulty, however, exists in any close alliance between Catholics and non-Catholics. This was most aptly illustrated as it was rather tartly expressed in a letter which I have quoted in my previous writing, from a non-Catholic woman who appealed to me for advice. This dear lady hoped that, being a convert, and having been a non-Catholic spouse in a mixed-marriage, I might be able to suggest a way to promote the harmony of her unsuccessful attempt to keep bachelor quarters with another young lady who happened to be a faithful Catholic.

Here is what her letter says: "There are many things in the Roman Church that attract me to it, but the unbending attitude of being completely right and brooking no disagreement with its teachings is intolerance of the worst kind and far from a Christian attitude."

Her expression of this grievance sets it forth in what might be called its pure state, because it was made in the face of the obvious easy remedy of breaking the alliance and finding another house-guest whom she would not need to bend.

It therefore brings into relief the tragic need for a better understanding of the nature of the difference when the same circumstance confronts the non-Catholic spouse of a mixed marriage. There the situation is aggravated to the Nth degree because it is specifically a perpetual and exclusive alliance. It is promised before God that the non-Catholic will not only refrain from trying to bend the Faith of the Catholic, but will allow all children born of the marriage to be baptized and educated as Catholics.

That this difficulty constitutes the poison of mixed marriage for the non-Catholic partner, and a tragic danger to the Catholic partner, I can vouch for from my own experience on both sides of the fence. That it is a difficulty largely because it is misunderstood on both sides, I can also vouch for from my own experience and from many, many interviews with others in similar circumstances.

The fact of misunderstanding is perhaps best illustrated by a quotation from another non-Catholic correspondent who insisted that she; and I quote: "simply cannot swallow what I don't believe the way most converts have to do." She still fails to realize how tragically funny such a conclusion is when one knows the real reason why the situation is a difficulty.

In almost every case it springs from a misunderstanding of the motive for Faith and the source of the doctrine. Very many non-Catholics in mixed marriages look upon the doctrine and the laws which bind their Catholic spouses as a code which has been drawn up by a long line of astute legislators who, through almost two thousand years of manipulation, have learned from experience how to keep their followers in complete subjection by the psychological bondage of fear.

Unfortunately, there are also enough Catholic spouses whose ignorance of the foundation of their own faith gives occasion for the confirmation of this conviction. The inevitable result is doubt, then loss of faith, gloom, unhappiness, and spiritual disaster for the entire family.

None of this need happen if the Catholic positively knows the fallacy in this perverted notion regarding the source of the Catholic Faith. As a matter of fact, even the non-Catholic should be able to sense the obvious truth which was presented by the Pharisee Gamaliel to his confreres of the Jewish Sanhedrin. Gamaliel's warning was given with respect to the very first of those so-called astute legislators, St.

Peter, after he had convinced three thousand converts in one day, that it was not he whose doctrine they were asked to believe, but that of Jesus of Nazareth who had proved by His life, His doctrine, and His Resurrection, that He was almighty God.

Gamaliel reminded the Jewish doctors of the Law: "Men of Israel, be cautious how you propose to act with regard to these men. . . . Because if this design or movement be from men it will be wrecked; but if it is from God you will not be able to put them down; and perhaps you may even find yourselves in conflict with God." (Acts 5:35-39).

That was nineteen hundred years ago. Yet many more thousands of the people who had witnessed the events that preceded and accompanied the founding of the Church by Jesus of Nazareth, and even though He was crucified as a malefactor, believed that He had proved Himself to be God. For that reason alone, they placed themselves under the guidance of the ministers whom they knew that Christ had chosen. These ministers were authorized and commanded by Christ to teach them the way of life and the form of worship which He wished them to follow. They did this in spite of the most bitter opposition and the determination to exterminate them on the part of the civil authorities. Their reason for doing so was, as they said: "We must obey God rather than men." (Acts 5:29).

The testimony of Gamaliel has been proven a thousand times in the nineteen hundred years since that event. The opposition has taken a thousand different forms, but the people ever since that day have continued to place themselves under the guidance of the successors of Peter for the same sole reason that it was God who told Peter: "He who receives anyone whom I send receives Me; and he who receives Me receives Him who sent Me." (John

God's Law and Man's Law

13:20). And He promised that: "The Holy Spirit whom the Father will send in My Name, He will teach you all things and will remind you of all that I have told you." (John 14:26). And, clinching it for all time, He had commanded and promised: "Go, therefore, and make disciples of all nations, . . . teaching them to observe all whatever I have commanded you and lo, I am with you all days even to the consummation of the world." (Matt. 28:19).

In all these years the acceptance of this doctrine and the continuance of confidence in it, hinges solely on the conviction that it is certain only because it is guaranteed by the promise of God. And, being from God, it cannot be divided but must be accepted or rejected in its totality. As a matter of fact, the nature of the doctrine is so high above the mentality of the natural man that the words of Gamaliel are obvious, that it never would have survived if it had not been from God rather than from man.

The pressure of man's natural inclination to divide Christ's Deposit of Faith and choose only what he pleases, has shown itself all down the centuries. And so it came about a little over four hundred years ago, that many people began to believe that the teaching authority established by Christ had ceased to fulfill the promises of Christ that it would not fail. They maintained that individual private judgment was the only criterion of religious truth as to the way of life and the form of worship commanded by God.

People ever since have continued to ally themselves with those who deny the certainty of the fulfillment of Christ's promises. *Their* acceptance of *this* belief and their continuance in it, hinges solely upon their conviction of the *un*-certainty of the truth of the doctrines with which they choose to disagree.

So, it should be obvious to the non-Catholic as well as to the wavering Catholic that an unbending attitude is not confined to either side, nor is it a question of one being all right and the other all wrong. Most Protestant Churches teach much of what the Catholic Church teaches. But the difference as to all of it is that the former is presented for acceptance on the authority of men; the latter has no shred of claim for preference unless it is accepted on the authority of God-Revealing.

But now comes the whole point of this lengthy explanation. There is no middle ground between these two positions. One cannot hold both views at the same time because they are incompatible with each other. That they are incompatible hinges, not upon the fact that *what* Catholics believe can never change, and *what* non-Catholics believe is always subject to what they call "the evolution of doctrine." No. The source of incompatibility is found in the reason *why* each believes as he does.

As a matter of fact, both agree that as to each question of doctrine there can be only one answer that is correct, and as to each item of God's law, there can be only one true statement of it. Truth and error do not admit of compromise. But it is intrinsic to all Protestant religion that each individual must select for himself, by the exercise of reason, the answer to each question of Faith or Morals. He must also constantly review his selections as the weight of opinion may accumulate against his previous decision.

It is intrinsic to the Catholic religion, that before one can become a member, he must satisfy himself that the answers to all questions of Faith or Morals are contained in a Deposit of Faith which has been revealed by God and has been entrusted to a Custodian established by God Himself and endowed with infallible protection against any change or error. Since the only reason for believing any of it

God's Law and Man's Law 51

is God's promise that it is all infallibly true, it is all or none. If a Catholic should doubt to the point of real disbelief, one item that God has placed in the Deposit of Faith, he becomes thereby a Protestant. He may continue to believe all the rest, but reason for belief becomes that of the Protestant, his own private judgment, not that of the infallible teaching authority established by God.

The convert, far from swallowing what he does not believe, has found the best possible reason for believing with more firm conviction than is ever possible for any of the faith of the non-Catholic. God is his backer!

The Protestant may consistently "bend" his opinion from time to time, but he should see that with the Catholic it is not a question of being bending or unbending: it is a question of being a Catholic or not being one. The situation would be entirely different if the authority for the faith of the Catholic were any one else than God.

So, with all this further explanation we should now be able to see that, even though marriage between baptized persons is a Sacrament and so, in the absence of mortal sin, gives husband and wife a special Sacramental Grace or power to meet successfully every problem of married life, still the situation in mixed marriages is fraught with untold difficulty and danger. The chief source of this danger is the difference in the understanding as to the motive for goodness. For the Catholic, the motive should be solely the Will of God and His glory. For the Protestant, no matter how holy, the motive can only be one's reasoned conviction as to the prescriptions of a proper moral code.

In these days, the atmosphere of Materialism has obviously contaminated the respect of the civilized world for the sanctity of Marriage. So it can hardly be expected that the non-Catholic party to a mixed marriage will approach this sacred union of souls with a purpose very different from that which moves one to make any other contract planned for the mutual satisfaction of the parties.

Certainly, it is often entered by non-Catholics without regard to the primary notion that it a holy and sacred vocation before God which must be worked at in a spirit of Charity and self-sacrifice for the principle purpose—one might say the only purpose worth mentioning—of making candidates for heaven out of the bride and groom and the children whom God may allow them the privilege of joining Him in giving the treasure of life.

The most tragic, and tragically the most widespread evidence of this gross disparity of appreciation of the sacredness of the married state, manifests itself in the sinful limitation of families, in defiance of God's will, so commonly practiced by husbands and wives.

God's law in this matter can be known by man without revelation and without grace. Man's intellect shows him the notes of human nature with which God has encompassed his being. His intellect also discloses that the continuity of all animate nature on the face of the earth depends upon the sexual appetite which God has placed in all animate nature. He then observes that the note of human nature which distinguishes it from all other animate nature is that the human being is the only one which is free from compulsion in the exercise of the law of his nature. Man's conscience, which is a part of the equipment of his intellect, then discloses that the satisfaction of the sexual appetite while intending the frustration of the purpose of it, is a sinful violation of the law of his nature, which is the law of God.

Father Francis J. McGarrigle has made a pertinent comment on man's unique privilege of freewill. He says: "Why man has been given the power of freely choosing sin is relatively plain. God wishes glory given to Himself not merely by necessity of imposed natural laws which cannot be frustrated; He desires also the glory that arises from a mind consciously glorifying Him and from a heart freely loving and obeying Him. To make man free to choose moral good or evil, is to make it possible for man to sin." (My Father's Will p. 115).

And so it is not the knowledge that it is sinful that makes the difference, but it is the appraisal of the enormity of this detestable depravity which steps in to degrade the souls of spouses and converts into lust of the lowest order the holy privilege which has been entrusted to them by God. A Catholic or non-Catholic husband who honestly loves his wife could hardly cast aside all respect for her sacred love, even on purely human grounds!

If, however, one makes one's self vulnerable to the temptation to commit this sin, whether Catholic or non-Catholic, three sources of obstacles immediately furnish abundant fuel with which to sear one's conscience. There is probably no other mortal sin which has such a large and out-spoken body of advocates. Furthermore, most of the advocates are highly "respectable" people. They feel safe in their advocacy because of their numbers. In fact, they can now point to the eminently respectable College of Bishops of the Church of England whose endorsement of the practice is only qualified by the stipulation that it be: "mutually acceptable to husband and wife in Christian conscience."

This stipulation insinuates the second obstacle to conformity to the law of God, namely: polite disagreement with the wisdom of the law. Volumes of quotations could be assembled to show that the strict observance of this law has been, or would have been, the cause of untold suffering if not the partial extinction of large portions of the human race by starvation. The inference being: therefore it cannot be the law of God.

One is reminded of the warning of Saint Paul: "For there shall come a time when people will not endure the sound doctrine; but having itching ears, they will in accordance with their own desires, accumulate teachers to themselves, and will turn away their ears from the truth, and stray off after fictions." (2 Tim. 4:3).

The delegates of the Lambeth Conference, never having laid claim to any authority beyond the opinion of the majority, have found themselves forced to yield the position which they themselves maintained as lately as 1920, and to bow to the will of those who have accumulated for themselves teachers in accordance with their own desires. In fact, emboldened by their success in accumulating opinion to suppress any qualms of conscience, they speak with patronizing contempt of those who prefer to allow God the whole responsibility for avoiding disaster to the human race which they say would result from universal obedience to His law.

The advocates of this denial of God's law often justify their claim by asserting that continued loving union between spouses is "impossible" without complete freedom as to sexual desire. Now every married person with any sense at all of human dignity knows in the depths of his or her heart that such an assertion is a detestable lie. And those who have practiced long periods of continence know that the exact opposite is true. Sacrifice for a loved one is a far greater source of respect and devotion than is any sharing in excessive indulgence. It is unfortunate that celibate priests find themselves hesitant to flatly contradict that detestable lie!

So, the pressure of these obstacles has made the avenue of reason and conscience to be the "hard way" to know the law of God. It has even diverted the unthinking advocate into referring to it as an exclusive law of the Catholic Church, thus appearing to lessen the pressure on conscience for those outside the Fold. But these overlook the unmistakable judgment of God expressed a thousand years before Christ or the Catholic Church came on the scene. When Onan made himself guilty of unnatural birth prevention, as reported in the thirty-eighth chapter of the Book of Genesis: verses 8-10; God punished him with death, not as a new expression of God's will, but because Onan knew that he had committed a detestable sin. And the objection to this interpretation of God's reason for punishing Onan is refuted by Deuteronomy 25:9 which states that a rejected widow may spit in the face of the culprit who refuses to take her for his spouse. Humiliating, perhaps, but a far cry from a sentence of death.

Three thousand years later the law of God is still the same and the violation of it is still a mortal sin. God has, however, changed the situation very much by providing what we have called the "easy way" to know His law. He has given us a Church which He has endowed with infallible knowledge of His law and He has commanded this Church to teach *all* men, not just those who find the law to their liking. But, being infinitely just, God has not left it to chance for men to find this easy way. He has made it possible for every man to identify this Church and He stands ready to aid with grace all men of good will, in or out of the Fold.

Now, it is quite possible that each reader of this chapter knows of a situation for which my comments seem to offer no solution. You may have talked with Catholic priests who have discussed this phase of the Problem of Evil in a different way. I beg you, however, not to draw the conclusion that my treatment of this subject reflects my ignorance of the fact that this is perhaps the most grievous obstacle to the Catholic Faith, and the most grievous test of the faithful to be found in the world today. On the contrary, that is precisely the reason why I have felt bound to discuss it at length. It is the outstanding example of the *danger to souls resulting from confused faith and wholesale bad example!*

The truth is that I have suffered with souls over this problem throughout my life as a priest. I have prayed over it. I have consulted with many theologians. I have dealt with trials of various kinds that seemed to make compromise with God's adorable will almost a necessity. But, the longer I live the more I am convinced that the only safe road to peace and happiness in this world and constant hope of infinitely greater safety as the hour of death approaches, is complete conformity to the will of God—*come what may*.

My experience has been that when one adheres with his whole soul to that conviction, God will never let him down. Whenever a soul in trouble with sin or doubt, will turn to me and say: "If that is God's will, Father, that is all I want to know. God's will be done!"—God will invariably flood that soul with an excess of peace, calm, love, joy—no matter how dark the worldly situation may appear to be. When the consequences of doing God's will are left entirely in God's hands, He always makes them good for the soul who trusts Him. Not only does He give grace to meet temptation, but, sin being put out of the question, temptation almost always vanishes with it.

There is, however, no situation and no soul to whom the compassion of Christ does not extend. Every priest is sent to be Christ's instrument to bring this compassion to souls. With God all things are possible. There is no single soul excluded from His grace. Devotion to all those virtues which reign in the Divine Heart of Jesus can be achieved by all those who learn to be aware of God's indwelling presence in every soul in a state of grace and His infinite love for each and every soul as if He and you were all-in-all. Our purpose in writing this chapter is to bring that kind of sunshine into every heart, not only of those who read it, but those with whom we live and those whom our example may inspire.

CHAPTER VI

THY WILL BE DONE

In a previous chapter we have discussed natural or human faith arrived at by means of sense perception and the use of the power of reason. We have compared it with supernatural or Divine Faith arrived at by examination of the evidence furnished by God to make ourselves eligible for the gift from God of the grace of the Supernatural Virtue of Faith.

Before we can expect this deep and abiding Faith to plunge us into love with God, there is one item of that faith which we must know for sure, and that, on a supernatural basis. We must know precisely what is meant by—The Will Of God. To know anything about God's will we must remember that, "The secrets of the Spirit of God have to be judged spiritually." In learning what is meant by God's will we will also come to know what is meant by the love which is the Virtue of Charity.

Saint Paul, in his first letter to his Corinthian converts, urges them to make use of that treasure of Faith resulting from the indwelling Spirit of Christ. He reminds them that they who have received this gift are no longer bound by the limitations of the "Natural Man". He says: "The natural man does not grasp the secrets of the Spirit of God, for they are folly to him; and he is unable to comprehend them because they have to be judged spiritually." Well, right now, in the study of the will of God and the meaning of the love which is Charity, we must exhibit our capacity for judging spiritually or else start all over again from the very beginning in order to learn to do so. The *word* love itself embraces concepts that are such poles apart that it furnishes a prime example of the need for being judged spiritually, and of the need to remember that the "secrets of the Spirit of God" are folly to the natural man.

I have a dear friend who would apparently really sincerely like to believe in the Catholic Faith. But his difficulty is that he could only believe it on his own terms, rather than those which we believe to be laid down by God. He is a psychiatrist and a scholar and has studied most of the modern schools of philosophy. He spent considerable time in Europe studying under Dr. Jung, one of the pioneers of Protestant psychiatry.

I had correspondence with him about the Faith in the earlier days of my conversion when I assumed that every scholarly person would certainly accept the Faith if only they could be made to understand it. I of course forgot that I myself had refused an open invitation to it for over twenty years.

I had sent him a copy of the book: "Christ, the Life of the Soul," written by the saintly Abbot Marmion, thinking it would give him a good introduction to the Faith in terms that were not too technical. His reply has had me meditating ever since: "The book," he wrote, "is only words to me, and worse, words and concepts which repel me, I suppose because I can't understand them. The concept of God loving Himself infinitely. What business have we with such a concept? That is an intellectualization and it came, I believe, from man's mind, not God's inspiration. If it is true, it is meaningless to us, or I should say to me."

For the past twenty years I have wondered how one should set out to explain the truth of God's love and God's will to the natural man *without* repelling him. Of course the difficulty lies in the impossibility of *having* human concepts which can embrace the reality of the utterly simple essence of God, not to mention the difficulty of expressing them in words.

This is understandably a stumbling-block to the natural man to whom the theandric concept of God existing somewhere in space smugly admiring Himself and His works with infinite satisfaction is perhaps justifiably repellent!

The man who judges spiritually, however, knowing that it is impossible for man to comprehend the infinite lovableness of God, does not for that reason, find it repellent to try to go as far as this so-called intellectualization will take him toward utilizing, for the good of his soul, what he knows to be true, from God's own revelation about Himself.

In fact, without some such attempt, he cannot hope to approach a proper attitude of adoration and worship of God for "taking the trouble" to create the universe and himself at all. The phrase "taking the trouble", is a feeble attempt to find words to indicate the graciousness of the free act of God's will which benefitted man, one might say, infinitely, since it is the difference between existence and nothingness, and yet it was utterly unavailable to add anything to God's blessedness.

Then, when man does begin to realize the gratitude he owes to God for creation, his gratitude is simply overwhelmed with humility when he learns that, after man in effect originally spit in God's face in thanks for creation, God showed His love for His creature by promising him a second chance.

The spiritual man also begins to realize that God's love for man is simply God's recognition of the partial perfection which God has put into this creature of His Will. God loves man as a faint reflection of the infinity of His own perfection.

By this time, the spiritual man is beginning to get a fragmentary, though intensely powerful sense of the necessity of the infinite love which goes with the oneness of God's Being. Even man can see that there

Thy Will Be Done

can be only one Infinite, which does not have parts, but *is* what we can only express by separate words.

So it is not repellent to him to see that love, will, knowledge, immensity, eternity, omnipotence, infinity, are all one in the pure Spirit, distinct from all creation, who is God. It would be just as impossible for God to be God without being infinite Love of Himself as it would be for Him to be God without being infinite Knowledge of Himself, the only Necessary Being.

After all, we do have very definite *business* with these concepts. For, in Christ, we are adopted sons of God the Father and in the present dispensation we do have God with us in the tabernacle, loving His partners in the Trinity with an infinite love, and loving each one of us with a love as real and intimate as if He had done all this for each one of us alone.

But this brings us back to the spiritual man who is floored by the contemplation of the utterly unnecessary act of the free will of God in creating man and in giving him a second chance after the disgrace of his Fall. In this state of humility the spiritual man then discovers the manner in which God willed to bring about this reinstatement or Redemption. Here he is faced by the revealed truth that God did what would be utterly unbelievable if it were not known from God Himself.

The story of the Incarnation owes much of its evidence to the fact that, humanly speaking, it is so unbelievable that even the eye-witnesses could not believe it in all its reality until they had proof heaped upon proof that God had done this thing.

It is so unbelievable that it could not possibly have been thought up or imagined by men. No man would ever have the temerity to try to convince another man that the infinite Triune Creator of the universe would respond to man's ingratitude and malice by foregoing even momentarily the exclusive enjoyment of His infinite Beatitude to take upon Himself the nature of the ungrateful creature for whom He had made the universe.

And so, the spiritual man, faced with the fact that God did just that, begins to have some idea of the generosity of God in freely willing to create man and the universe for the purpose of enabling man to enjoy the manifestation of God's glory. But he is still more impressed by the infinite power of God's will to effectuate His purpose, even though man seemed to come so near to spoiling it all, that only God, Himself become Man, could right the wrong.

So it begins to dawn upon the spiritual man, or rather, God begins to give him the grace to understand that every act of the adorable generosity of God Incarnate is done in conformity with the will of God the Father by whom He was sent. "I have descended from heaven, not to do My own will, but the will of Him who sent Me." (John 6:38).

We know that God could have redeemed man without the humiliation of taking our human nature and yet Christ has told us that it was "necessary" that the Son of Man should come into the world and should suffer all these indignities, even the torturing, by His unworthy creatures, of His death upon the Cross. Why, then, was it necessary? Solely because it was the will of God to fulfill His purpose in that manner.

"For this purpose I have been born and for this purpose I have come into the world—to bear witness to the truth." (John 18:37).

"And He began to teach them that the Son of Man must endure many sufferings and be rejected by the ancients, chief priests and scribes, and be put to death and after three days rise again." (Mark 8:31)

Thy Will Be Done

Not only were these great and unprecedented events of the Incarnation done in complete conformity with the purpose of the will of God, but as Christ Himself tells us, every act of His life was done to fulfill the will of His Father. Of course, Christ's will *was* the will of God, but He had a human will which rebelled at the indignities which He was called upon to suffer. He was steadfast in subjecting His human will to the will of His Father, even against all human advice, as when Saint Peter attempted to dissuade Him: "But He . . . reprimanded Peter, saying, 'Go behind Me Satan! For thou art thinking not according to God, but according to man.'" (Mark 8:33).

If Christ, our God and divine Savior, modeled every act of His life in conformity to the will of His Father, how much more should we, realizing our utter dependence upon Him, also realize the folly and malice of opposing our puny wills to His. God made it so plain that our only good is to do His will that no man of "Good Will" can fail to be aware of it.

We, who are at least beginning to have the grace to judge spiritually, can easily see that human self-love which centers on creatures and detaches the human will from the Creator, is poles apart from spiritual self-love which centers upon union with God and our neighbor, and which God commands us to foster.

God commands this because the relationship between God and ourselves and our neighbor is a faint reflection of the relationship of infinite spiritual love existing within the Holy Trinity between the Father, Son and Holy Spirit. We can see that this love and respect for ourselves and our neighbors which is due from us, is a recognition of the adoration to which God is entitled for willing our existence in His image and for keeping us in existence from moment to moment.

God's infinite mercy and patience which exceeds the possibility of our comprehension, begins to be apparent when we realize that man has been by far the greatest beneficiary of God's will in all creation. Yet, with the possibile exception of the rebellious angels, man has probably been the least docile to His will.

In the first chapter of the Book of Genesis we read these words: "And God saw all that He had made and found it very good." (Gen. 1:31). It gives us pause to realize that no material creature manifested any resistance to God's will until man came on the scene—man the creature for whom all the rest was made. God willed it all without the slightest benefit to Himself except the pleasure of imparting this blessing upon man—this creature whom God had made in His image.

This reflection of God's image in man is his capacity to perceive God's goodness, and acknowledge his dependence upon God and freely adhere to God's will which he can know.

It gives us still greater pause to then recall that even when man perverts the use of the free-will God has given him, he still does fulfill God's infinite purpose, to his own tragic ruin. This is the awful thought that gives birth to Saint Paul's admonition to: "Work out your salvation with fear and trembling." (Phil. 2:12). God's eternal purpose in creation did obviously include the Fall of Man. From that stems all the evil that God has allowed in accordance with His purpose. We do not know precisely *why* it is included in God's purpose; perhaps because, but for that, the objective reality of man's free will would not be so obvious. Neither would God's love be so obviously manifested in those who

Thy Will Be Done

fulfill His purpose by union with His will. The Problem of Evil will involve some mystery until the end of time.

We know for sure, however, that when God finished His original work of creation, everything was "very good" because it was the glorious manifestation of His will. He endowed men and angels alone with intellect and will, those qualities which most nearly reflect His infinite perfection. Both did abuse this power and their "happy fault" manifested all of God's lovableness in the Incarnation and Redemption.

"For He made known to us the mystery of His will, the free design which He had determined to carry out in the fullness of time—namely, to bring back all things both in the heavens and on the earth under the headship of Christ." (Eph. 1:10). We can realize faintly the immensity of Christ's love for those who in Him have obtained the inheritance predestined according to the purpose of His will, when we meditate on what He went through for them. We should also remember that it is to increase the perfection of those whom He has predestined to conform to His will, that He has permitted those to be born who by their own fault have resisted His will and merited reprobation. This emphasizes the preciousness of the elect. Not only did Christ suffer all He did for them, but for the refinement of their perfection, He permitted the awful evil of sin.

It is for us then, to choose whether Christ will continue to do the will of His Father in us by His union with our docile wills or, by our stupid natural self-love, we will make our souls inhospitable dwelling places for Him, where complete union of wills is lacking and where love will always be on trial. And where, even the danger of mortal sin will always lurk as a terrible possibility!

Hear what Saint Paul advises us: "Let us not become vain-glorious, provoking one another, envying one another. For the fruit of the spirit is love, gladness, peace, longsuffering, kindness, goodness, fidelity, mildness, continence." (cf. Gal. 5:22-26). "He who sows from the spirit shall from the spirit reap eternal life. And let us not grow weary in welldoing, for in due time we shall reap if we do not relax. So then, when we have opportunity, let us do good to all, but especially to those of the household of the Faith." (Gal. 6:8-10).

Our individual destiny is rightly all-important to us, but the best way to secure it is to always remember that we are a part of God's providence with respect to our neighbor. We can be made saints by the evil acts of our neighbor, but far more readily can we be made saints by wishing our neighbor well because God wishes them well and by freely cooperating with the will of God in perfecting the lives of others. As Father Francis McGarrigle remarks in his estimable book, *My Father's Will*: "Love of our neighbor is really conformity with God's will concerning man, and consequently it is love of God."

Christ has shown us beyond doubt that the purpose of our creation is the fulfillment of the perfect will of God in us, not only in the great events of our lives, but rather that no thought or word or act of ours is pleasing to God except insofar as it is His action in us. It is thus that we can all be other Christs, by allowing Him to live on in us, carrying out His mission to do the will of His Father in all things.

Even though He is God which we can never be, He gives us the privilege of participating in His divinity through the imitation of His Humanity in giving glory to God by uniting with His will. "I glorified Thee on earth by accomplishing the work

Thou gavest Me to do. And now do Thou Father glorify Me with Thy own Self." (John 17:4-5). Christ already possessed all the glory of His divine nature. It can only be in His Humanity that He asks this glory for Himself and for all those abiding in Him in union in all things with the divine will.

CHAPTER VII

FOOLS' GOLD
AND PROJECT SAINTHOOD

When I first became a Catholic convert, I was, in the ordinary parlance of the world, a "rich man". A thought that often crossed my mind was a sort of wondering fear of the words of Christ which so often seemed to place the rich, as such, beyond the pale of salvation. I often asked myself the question: Just what did Christ mean when He said: "I tell you further, it is easier for a camel to pass through the eye of a needle than for a rich man to enter the Kingdom of God." (Matt 19:24). Did Christ categorically exclude all the rich from His love when He said: "Woe to you who are rich! for you have received your consolation." (Luke 6:24). Was Christ speaking exclusively when He said to the "rich young man": "If thou desirest to be perfect . . . go, sell thy possessions and give to the poor, and thou shalt possess treasure in heaven; and come, follow Me!" (Matt. 19:21). Why should any one *not* desire to be perfect? Did Christ have no place in His heart for one who was neither poor, nor hungry, nor weeping, nor hated nor reviled? (cf Luke 6:20).

These texts frankly bothered me. They obviously needed interpretation. Taken literally, they made a fairly hopeless prospect for those whose industry and thrift, aided by good use of the faculties God had given them, had made them, to use the words of the Gospel, "the possessors of much wealth."

Christ seemed to exclude the possibility of retaining wealth and at the same time becoming His devoted follower—the kind of follower that every one who really learned to believe in Him would certainly want to be. In fact, the comparison of the camel

Fools' Gold and Project Sainthood 69

and the needle's eye was apropos of the rich young man who is described as having kept all the commandments from boyhood (cf Mark 10:20) and who apparently was a person of good will.

Like the rich young man of the Gospel, I sought advice in the matter and, like the rich young man, I turned away saddened by the advice I received. I was told that all the hearers of Christ knew that He was referring to the gate in the wall of the city of Jerusalem called the "Needle's Eye" which made His comment mean that it was truly difficult, but not impossible. I had my doubts. I had seen that gate when I was in Jerusalem five years before I became a Catholic. I had heard the same story then, but it had impressed me that this interpretation was not much help. Even a well-trained circus camel would have no chance to move if it crouched low enough to pass through that gate! Of course I also knew that the gate called the Needle's Eye in Jerusalem today could not have been the one referred to by Christ because Jerusalem was left without "a stone upon a stone" some thirty years after those words were spoken. So that was small consolation.

Another observation that did not help the situation was the general atmosphere of suspicion expressed even in the New Testament as to the legitimacy of wealth. How was the rich young man to find solace in this quotation from Saint James: "Come now, you rich, weep and wail over your impending miseries! Your wealth is rotten and your garments are moth-eaten. Your gold and silver are rusted and their rust shall become an evidence against you and shall consume your flesh like fire." (5:1-3).

Now all these disquieting thoughts apply to a big percentage of good Catholics today. Many of you have material possessions and comforts which would have placed you in the category of the "rich" as compared with those who made up the multitude who followed Christ and received the benedictions mentioned in His Sermon on the Mount. What would be our chances of being Christ's chosen friends? Could it be that He would not admit any one into the inner circle of His friendship unless they made themselves poor by giving away all their worldly goods?

This problem puzzled me for many years. Perhaps the ultimate solution I chose was the "easy way", namely, to step out from under the personal obligation of finding a general solution by subjecting myself to a Vow of Poverty.

But obviously that cannot be the only adequate solution of the problem for two very good reasons. First: If it is the only satisfactory solution, then every one should adopt it. But if every one did adopt it, the whole fabric of Christian society as it stands today would collapse. Second: Every faithful Christian today finds himself in a state of life which he has arrived at with the help of God's grace, and under complete control of God's Providence. For most people this means present obligations which would make it impractical if not immoral for them to completely divest themselves of property to avoid the opprobrium of being rich!

This makes it quite evident that what I have called the easy way which I have taken, is simply not available to many. And so most people are left in the same quandary in which I found myself before I could take the easy solution suggested by Christ, namely: "Sell all that thou hast and come, follow Me." My present state, however, coupled with this past experience should qualify me to help find a solution for those who are still in the situation which I once occupied, namely: rich in the goods of this world.

Fools' Gold and Project Sainthood

Now, as things stand today, this situation includes a wide range of people from the man or woman with a job and a good hourly wage, to the man whose annual income may be in the millions. It should enable me to give not only sound but understanding advice to the person, however situated, who is honestly conscientious about the problem of alms-giving.

Let us immediately then, settle the most important question of all: What was Christ's true attitude toward the rich? It can be safely said that Christ never intended to class the possession of wealth as such, as evil or immoral. He dealt with His hearers in a manner best calculated to make a lasting impression on the hearts of those who were before Him there and then. Being God, however, His words were also perfectly planned for the instruction of all men of all time to whom they would be reported.

So, let us see how this conclusion is justified, even with the seeming impossibility expressed in the statement about the camel and the needle's eye.

The Gospels of Matthew, Mark and Luke all report the same uncompromising words. In some manuscripts of Saint Mark's Gospel a ray of mitigation is contained in the words of Christ which preceed this condemnatory statement. Saint Mark quotes Christ as saying first: "Children, how difficult it is for those who *trust* in wealth to enter the Kingdom of God!" Elsewhere, the opprobrium is expressed against those who *cling* to riches. But even so, the statement which follows does not admit of an absolutely literal interpretation.

And so, as we look further we see that even the Apostles who had already left all things to follow Christ, were astounded and incredulous at this harsh-sounding statement, "saying to one another, 'Who, then, can be saved?'" (Matt. 19:26). Jesus then, answering their thoughts, gives us the clue. He says:

"With men this is impossible; but with God all things are possible." From this it can be understood that riches, as such, are not condemned, but rather, it is the plight of those possessors of wealth whose hearts are not responsive to the grace of God. For, after all, entrance into the Kingdom of God depends entirely upon the state of one's soul.

So, Christ's answer to the question of the Apostles: "Who can be saved?" might be interpreted to mean: None but those who cooperate with the supernatural gift of God's grace which God gives to whomsoever He will. Here the rich man is certainly at some disadvantage because his cooperation with grace is more likely to be opposed by what Christ called "the seduction of wealth" (Matt. 13:22) which He referred to in the parable of the sower as "choking the word and it becomes unproductive." It follows then that the rich man is not to be barred from heaven merely as a result of the possession of wealth. He is, however, solemnly warned that the manner of acquisition of wealth and the use of wealth both involve grave dangers and temptations which place the possessor of wealth in proximate danger of forgetting his utter dependence upon God.

Even Saint James' tirade against the rich, we find modified by the presupposition that it is both ill-gotten and mishandled, for he continues by saying: "See! The wages of the workmen fraudulently withheld by you, cry out . . . you have pampered your hearts in a day that reeked of slaughter." (James 5:4)

So the warning against the wealthy is not a hopeless one, but it should, nevertheless, give pause to all of us who have been blessed by God with a sufficiency of this world's goods lest we forget that it all belongs to God before it belongs to us so that we are accountable to God for the use of it.

The great scholar and interpreter of Scripture,

Fools' Gold and Project Sainthood

Father Andres Fernandez, S.J. gives us an encouraging clue as to the purpose of Christ in some of the apparently severe expressions of His teaching. In his book, *The Life of Christ*, he explains the parable of the camel and the needle's eye as follows: "Christ was speaking to an unlettered oriental crowd. Therefore He clothed His doctrine in language designed to hold their attention and convey His meaning. He used vivid imagery, striking phrases, hyperbole so bold that at times it bordered on the unlikely and even on the impossible. Take for example the sentence: "It is easier for a camel to pass through the eye of a needle, than for a rich man to enter the Kingdom of Heaven" (Matt. 19:24); or that maxim . . . "So if thy right eye is an occasion of sin to thee, pluck it out and cast it from thee . . ." (Matt. 5:29-30). Father Fernandez then continues: "The people were accustomed to this mode of expression and their common sense enabled them to grasp the lesson contained." (*Life of Christ, p.* 329)

And so this message of Christ is addressed to each one of us here today; for each one of us is a rich man or woman in the sense of Christ's meaning. It is of course most forceful in its application to those who have been blessed by God with more than ordinary abundance of the goods of this world. How then should we answer the question which immediately comes to the mind of those who are in a position to give alms and who honestly want to know: "What does Christ expect of me?"

In the first place, let me make this clearly understood: The answer is not to be named in dollars or in percentage of income or in comparison with what John Nabor has given or will give. The answer is measured in love. Each one of us has an obligation to Christ which is utterly impossible for us to satisfy.

There is no such thing as a just return on our side of the bargain with Christ because whatever we offer to Him our obligation remains infinite.

The point is that it is not the *amount* of our money or works of mercy that pleases Christ, but it is our motive for giving. If our motive springs from our recognition of our infinite obligation of gratitude to Christ our inclination will be to give and to do more than the world would consider prudent. But, to the extent that our motive is pure love of Christ, He will see to it that we do not suffer but rather that we profit immensely for any imprudence of this kind.

The more realistic our appreciation of our debt of gratitude to Christ, the stronger becomes the incentive to give ourselves and all that we have to Him. And the more we give, the more we receive from Him in return.

This marks the difference between the Catholic who knows his Faith and the philanthropist, whatever be his faith, who gives from a purely natural motive. The donation of the latter is called charity, but he does not come near the true meaning of the supernatural Virtue of Charity which stems only from Christ. He receives his reward, but as Christ reminds us through Saint Paul, his reward is the sounding brass and the tinkling cymbal of admiration and honor here and now. "And if I should distribute all my goods to feed the poor and if I should deliver my body to be burned and have not charity, it profiteth me nothing." (I. Cor. 13:3).

The former prefers the precious promise of Christ: "But when thou givest alms, do not let thy left hand know what thy right hand is doing so that thine almsgiving may be in secret; and thy Father who sees in secret will reward thee." (Matt. 6:3-4) . . . one hundredfold in this world and in the world to come life everlasting.

Fools' Gold and Project Sainthood

If the question of motive is solved, the question of amount will take care of itself. Each one in his present state can do all that Christ wishes him to do if he remembers that all that he has belongs to Christ. Each one is the custodian for Christ of a portion of the world's goods. He who loves these goods in preference to Christ will derive no benefit from them and is in grave danger of depriving himself entirely of Christ's love. In proportion as one loves Christ he will be detached from the love of wealth and will be disposed to use his wealth in accordance with the will of Christ.

Even one who has the greatest and healthiest enthusiasm for the use of this world's goods may still despise them in comparison with the love of Christ. The one who is seeking an opportunity to show his love for Christ will find joy in ministering his wealth for the benefit of those whom Christ loves. Christ has identified Himself with those in need. "Inasmuch as you have done it for one of the least of these My brethren you have done it unto Me." (Matt. 25:40).

It is this motive that is rewarded with treasure in heaven. And since heaven is forever, that reward is infinite. By the same token, the short-sighted spirit of avarice that makes one find excuses for turning away from the support of Christ's Church and Christ's poor, is penalized with an infinite loss.

What a tragedy of folly it will seem if one learns too late that the excuses he has contrived, to cling to his wealth and refuse the support needed by the Church and the poor, have cost him that reproach of Christ: "I was hungry and you gave Me no food; . . . I was sick and in prison and you visited Me not . . . for as long as you did not do so to one of these least, neither did you do so to Me." (Matt. 25:42-46).

The love of Christ is a precept of God. The use of wealth in acknowledgment of that precept is an obligation under pain of grave sin. But the Christian who begins to understand the meaning of the love of Christ will respond with a generosity that begins far beyond the horizon of the margin of sin.

Charity which is the love of God and the love of neighbor for the love of God, has no outer limit of application in this world or the next. This does not mean that everyone should despoil himself of worldly possessions to satisfy the precept to love God, but it does mean that sainthood is offered to the rich as well as to the poor provided they learn to know that the use of their wealth is their priceless opportunity to prove their love for God.

For those who are in a position to "leave all things to follow Christ", the invitation given to the rich young man still offers the opportunity for the most profitable investment that can be made in this world. For those whose state of life does not permit such action the true love of Christ will inspire a spirit of custodianship toward the possession of wealth that will yield a reward proportionate to that love.

If a true understanding of the gratitude we owe to Christ were the universal motive for alms-giving, no Pastor would ever have to bother you with "money talks". Instead, you would be bothering him with your generosity. You would be always crowding the upper limit of income-tax-deductible contributions, and with each contribution you would find yourself one hundred times more rich. You would constantly learn from experience that it is "more blessed to give than to receive." You would rejoice in the tender message of Saint John: "My little children, let us love, not in word nor with the tongue, but in act and in truth. By this we shall know that we are of the truth and shall tranquilize our hearts before Him." (I. John 3:18-20).

CHAPTER VIII
MORE BLESSED RECEIVERS

We have now devoted a chapter to the appraisal of the infinite treasure which God offers to those who are the givers of true Supernatural Charity. This might be taken to imply that no such bounty of treasure is available to those who must be the receivers of the works of supernatural charity. Pleas for charity often quote the words of Saint Paul in his exhortation to the bishops and clergy of Ephesus: "Remember the saying of the Lord Jesus, how He Himself said: 'It is more blessed to give than to receive.'" (Acts 20:35). And so I do indeed hasten to acknowledge the truth of these words while announcing the title of this chapter as, *More Blessed Receivers*. Please understand, however, that this title does not indicate my intention to refute these precious words of Our Lord, but rather to interpret them in a new light which I believe is more in keeping with Christ's meaning.

My reason for wishing to do this is twofold. First and foremost: I have what I believe is an important message for the vast majority of those who have little or no prospect of being "givers" in the sense of having an abundance of the goods of this world. Especially will this message be aimed at two extremes of this group: those who find humiliation in the necessity of receiving; and that vast throng of their opposites who have made receiving a vocation ever since those devastating days of the 1930's when politics encouraged men to mooch!

The second reason for my twofold purpose is to explain a sense in which the blessing in giving comes from that which it makes the giver receive; and a sense in which all receivers may be the greatest givers. If I succeed, even in part, every reader may be found in some category whereby each may become a "more blessed receiver."

So here is my message to the first of those apparent non-givers, those who find in poverty or sickness or helplessness of any kind, a terrible cross, not so much because it involves long hours of want and pain and waiting, but chiefly because it may involve dependence upon other human beings, especially those who may render the necessary service grudgingly and without Charity.

How common it is for us to dread that necessity of being helped by others. And here may I hint that often the worst offenders are those who belong to a category that includes a large percentage of adults; those who dread the approach of old age. Almost all of these people bristle, at least a little, against this necessity which they feel is a bruise to what they think of as self-respect. But it is not really the virtue of self-respect that generates this repugnance. Let's face it, the sense of injury usually stems from pride, that most common and most insidious of all those ills which beset fallen human nature.

Admittedly, however, this manifestation of pride in mental and physical competence is often made less culpable when it stems from so-called righteous anger against those who are always whining that nobody loves them, as an excuse for demanding attention from others when it is not really needed. The same righteous indignation is directed against those who simply contrive to impose upon others with deliberate selfishness or deceitful looting of the treasury of Charity.

It is true that Jesus Christ showed us that these practices aroused His righteous anger. Being God, however, He knew what was in the hearts of men, and could be sure of His accuracy when He said: "Woe to you, . . . hypocrites, for you devour the property of widows under the pretext of making long prayers; for which you shall receive a severer sentence." (Matt. 23:14). But His advice to us was: "Judge not, that you may not be judged. For according to the judgment you pronounce, you shall be judged, and with the measure you measure with, it shall be measured back to you." (Matt. 7:1-2).

And so, the art of receiving graciously can be a reflection of the acme of blessed Christian humility which is a very far cry from smarting under so-called humiliation. There are times of course when a rebuke to others might be merited either for a grudging response to a needed appeal or for whining or deceitful misrepresentation of a need. But the only worthy Christian motive for such a rebuke is to help the offender. This is almost never done by a harsh word to the grudging giver or by curt refusal to the whining mendicant. A grudging giver may be much more likely put to shame by a truly sincere expression of grateful appreciation.

So, my heartfelt and understanding and sympathetic suggestion to those who must be receivers in any way, is that they shun the thought of confusing humility with humiliation; that they try to realize the folly of pride in one who must be a receiver; that they remember that it is Christ who permits their needs even though He loves them perhaps more than those whom He does not chastise. It is by referring all things to Christ with a calm determination to love Him, come what may, that you can learn to be saints. So, when you are aging or when you are suffering in sickness or when you are victims of physical or material disability, remember that the road to sainthood is traveled most successfully by those who are more blessed receivers.

And now a word about those whom I have called the opposites of those who must receive because of some trial dispensed to them by the Providence of God: those who contrive some selfish advantage for themselves without giving anything of themselves in return. This, of course, includes all those who are doubtful beneficiaries of public welfare agencies, but is by no means confined to them. In fact, the wealthiest man in the city may and too often does place himself in this unenviable category. There are all too many who seek advantage for themselves at the expense of public welfare or the common good.

Starting with the professional burglar, smuggler, abortionist, counterfeiter, swindler, drug pusher and those who misuse the power to strike; society rebels against this class and fights to protect itself against them.

I have referred to this group in general as: "that vast throng who have made receiving a vocation." Naturally, the first candidates thought of are those who have brought about by their machinations the almost inhuman scrutiny that is often visited upon applicants for public welfare funds. These are indeed particularly evil. They are accountable not only for the true humiliation to which legitimate beneficiaries are subjected, but also for the elimination of the spirit of true charity from the hearts of those who would otherwise be loyal supporters of such agencies as are the recipients of funds from Community Chest campaigns.

These are no less pernicious than the tramp who studies the art of fiction to compose a lying hard-luck-story of hungry children and sick wife. The more realistically he succeeds in framing his story, the more profitable it becomes. It might almost be said that it would be less wicked to steal directly from the needy rather than to sour the hearts of

More Blessed Receivers

those who would otherwise give them more. These two classes of moochers, the professional criminals and the professional tramps, do not read my books; they do not come to retreats or listen to sermons, but every citizen has a moral duty to help to cure them because they, too, are sick members of society, every one of them, and they do need Christian help. The toll they take runs into the kind of figures that national debts are made of. Perhaps they serve some purpose because, if they were removed, this world would be so lovely that heaven would seem less to be sought after.

It is easy to recognize the evil done by these antisocial parasites, but let us not deceive ourselves, this costly selfishness is not confined to those who are admitted criminals. It seems that all of us have occasional urges toward selfish appropriation against the common good.

During the war-time it became more obvious when the worst offenders bragged about having ways to get more than their fair quota of sugar or shoes or gasoline. Others used the ability to give such privileges to ingratiate themselves with friends. They were cheating the soldiers who were fighting for their liberty.

But is it so very much less unchristian to carry the same tactics into peace time with all sorts of selfish practices and devices to secure special privilege or more than one's share by evasion of taxes or unjust use of authority in dozens of other ways: to give jobs to those who do not deserve them; to strike to prevent the use of labor-saving equipment; to promote a boycott for purely selfish aims; to become, or make someone else a receiver at the expense of someone for whom a job or goods were intended?

Most of us should study to make our consciences a little more tender in recognizing the selfishness in some of the things we do, sometimes thoughtlessly, to gain an advantage for ourselves. The goods or privileges we receive in this manner by no means tend to make us blessed receivers!

Now for my message to the givers and receivers who may change by their intentions the maxim of Christ that it is more blessed to give than to receive.

First, to those givers who spoil by their motive any blessedness which Christ has planned for them. Christ Himself mentions some of these, for example: "When, therefore, thou givest alms, do not have a trumpet blown before thee, as the hypocrites do in the synagogues and in the streets, that they may be honored by men. Indeed, I tell you, they have received their reward! But when thou givest alms do not let thy left hand know what thy right hand is doing, so that thine almsgiving may be in secret; and thy Father who sees in secret will reward thee." (Matt. 6:2-4).

In other words, the only kind of giving that is a source of blessedness or sainthood is that which is inspired solely by a love of God and a desire to give proof of that love by "taking it out on our neighbor." That is: "Thou shalt love thy neighbor as thyself for the love of God."

This applies to absolutely every kind of giving whether it be in alms or corporate works of mercy or spiritual works of mercy. It applies to the philanthropist and the founder of great charitable foundations as well as to the humble preacher or religious who gives his whole life for the benefit of souls.

It is only blessed if it is done as evidence of love of God. It does not follow that to preach for a living is sinful, but it has no merit with God unless it reflects His love. Neither is it sinful to give to charity in order to be honored by men, but how very puny is the reward compared with that which comes from

God. "And if I give bit by bit all my possessions to feed the poor, but not for the love of God, it would avail me nothing." (I. Cor. 13:3).

That is, the honor and acclamation of men is "nothing" compared with the blessedness which God gives to those who go all-out to do all that they do to show Him their love.

It is this contamination of worldly motive which has destroyed the spirit of Charity in many of our modern money-raising campaigns. Our Community Chests and fund-raising drives too often emphasize only the motive of competition in being seen by men to be honored by them. The result is usually the unwilling and grace-starved sparse giver so aptly compared by Saint Paul with the giver enlightened by love: "He who sows sparingly shall also reap sparingly, and he who sows bountifully shall also reap bountifully. Let each one give as he has determined in his heart, not with reluctance or from compulsion; for God loves a cheerful giver." (II. Cor. 9:7).

And here again I return to my thesis: What makes cheerful giving blessed is the overwhelming flood of receiving which always accompanies the love which begets the cheer. "He who forsakes his possessions for My Name's sake shall receive one hundredfold in this world and inherit life everlasting." (Matt. 19:29). And so the cheerful giver who gives for the love of God—"for My Name's sake" becomes at once a more blessed receiver.

And now to return to the first group mentioned: those who are chosen by God to be necessary receivers, and to show how they may become the most blessed of all by being the givers of that which has the greatest value with God.

I know of such a one and have prayed for him every day for many years. His trifling little handicap is that from birth he has been without hands or feet, only little vestiges of the limbs that God gives to the rest of men. Without constant human aid he simply could not live. Yet, he has not only lived but has supported himself and a frail brother whose heart condition makes him unable to work. He has done it by an indomitable will and the exploitation in various ways of his greatest asset, a good clear mind and voice.

The condescending reluctance of the wrong kind of giver and the contriving deception of the wrong kind of receiver have stirred up in him a horror of becoming a receiver who cannot give quid pro quo. But, by no less than a miracle of grace, God let him see that his example of complete abandonment to the will of God under conditions which might daunt the holiest of men, could make him a giver on a scale that would belittle every worldly fortune that men can have.

And so it may become a gift with every one who seems to suffer from that inscrutable Providence of God that manifests itself in the Problem of Evil and makes some men to be unwilling receivers of the corporal works of mercy. By the alchemy of God's love they may become the greatest givers, and hence the most blessed receivers of all.

Again Saint Paul reminds us: "For power is perfected in weakness. Rather therefore will I gladly boast of my weaknesses that the power of Christ may rest upon me. Therefore I take pleasure in infirmities, in persecutions, in difficulties for the sake of Christ, for when I am weak, then I am strong." (II. Cor. 12:9-10).

This idea is neatly expressed in a narrative sketch of the retreat movement fostered by the Religious of the Cenacle for all kinds of people who suffer infirmities. The author of the narrative reports: "But perhaps the most profoundly moved by the experience of a retreat are the Alcoholics Anonymous. They may be said in truth to give more than they receive, such is the impact of their enthusiasm and appreciation upon the religious who minister to them." (*Women of the Cenacle*, p. 133).

And so it is with every act of mercy. There must be receivers in order that God may bless the givers, but the true spirit of Charity on both sides makes it impossible to specify which is which and, in the long run, God makes every one most blessed as a receiver of His love!

CHAPTER IX

OUR FATHER WHO ART IN HEAVEN

Perhaps it is well in this mid-chapter to refer again to our opening chapter entitled: *Deliver Us From Evil*. The theme of this book is to rejoice over the perfection of God's reign over the world. But, one item of that perfection involves the liberty of man's free-will which, in these days, has made it necessary to shout to every man, woman and child, the utter disaster that endangers all mankind as a result of the assault of Atheism and Materialism on *Supernatural Faith* in our world. The true notion of the necessity of prayer is being crowded out of our mentality by the wholesale example of supernatural blindness and the godless behavior which it generates. The world is becoming blind to the source and meaning of these words: *Our Father who art in heaven, Hallowed be Thy name, Thy Kingdom come, Thy Will be done on earth as it is in heaven.* (Matt. 6:9-10)

To be honest with you, I chose this text only after spending a good deal of thought on the obvious: "I believe in God the Father Almighty, Creator of heaven and earth." I also toyed with several other ideas, chief of which was Deuteronomy 6:4-7: "Hear, O Israel, the Lord thy God is one Lord. Thou shalt love the Lord thy God with thy whole heart, and with thy whole soul, and with thy whole strength. And these words which I command thee this day shall be in thy heart: and thou shalt meditate upon them sitting in thy house, and walking on thy journey, sleeping and rising." I also considered these words from the Athanasian Creed: "The Person of the Father is distinct, the Person of the Son is distinct, the Person of the Holy Spirit is distinct. But of the Father and of the Son and of the Holy Spirit the Divinity is One, the Glory equal, the Majesty coeternal. As the Father is, such is the Son and such is the Holy Spirit." (*Apologetics*, Vol. II, p. 11).

As a matter of fact, I want to study with you our Faith in God the Father almighty in the light of all these texts. The reason I have chosen the first twenty-four words of the Lord's Prayer as the basis of this chapter stems from my admiration—I might almost say, my adoration, of the perfection with which these words of God Himself embrace what might be called "the whole law and the prophets."

They give us a pattern of perfection derived from the most fundamental item of our Faith, namely: that God our Creator, the All-Holy Moulder of our destiny and Commander of our existence, is also our loving Father who by the amazing ingenuity of the Incarnation of His Son, through the power of the Holy Spirit, has made us heirs to real sonship, real participation in the blessedness of His Divinity which would otherwise be utterly beyond the possibility of hope.

The readers of my other books know that I am always dragging in a plug for what I have tried to make the theme of my life and the motive of every thought and word and act: the prayer of adoration put on our lips by God Himself: "Thy will be done!" And this motto fits perfectly with the conclusions which I wish to draw as a sequel to the consideration of our bare faith in God the Father almighty.

Does it ever puzzle you to advert to the fact that the most absolutely basic item of our faith is a mystery which is utterly beyond the possibility of human comprehension? I mean the Trinity of Persons in God. Time, the world, and eternity are explained in terms of a God of three Persons and one Divine Nature. The Trinity is God, and Its action is always expressed by a singular verb. And yet the Father who is God is not the Son who is God and neither of them is the Holy Spirit who is God.

But the Athanasian Creed plainly states that: "Whoever wishes to be saved must, before all things. . . . worship one God in Trinity and Trinity in unity." Our futile finite attempt to thoroughly grasp this idea reminds me of the trick of language which brings it about that there is a meaningful short sentence in English which can be perfectly understood when spoken but which cannot possibly be put in writing. The sentence is this: There are three twos (to's too's) in the English language.

But while that sentence is truly impossible to write and the former is truly impossible for us to comprehend in its entirety, our salvation is not thereby completely lost because it is altogether possible for us to believe it even though we cannot comprehend it. In fact, it should be altogether easy for us to believe it for the sole reason that we have other ways of knowing that God has told us that it is true.

There is perhaps one clue on the natural plane to help us to understand the necessity of this supernatural mystery. If God did become Man in the Person of Christ, He must have a nature which is not confined to the human body of Christ but is still in command of the universe. In other words, the Man Christ must have two natures, the divine one being united to a divinity functioning as it had from all eternity, the human one being the abode of the Godhood of the Person of God. On the other hand, if unity limited Godhood to God the Father, Creator and Preserver of the universe, the unbelievably beautiful means of Redemption by the Incarnation would have been impossible. And equally, though less obviously impossible would be the Sanctification of souls by the indwelling Spirit of God.

There is, however, a flaw in this clue since we know, also by revelation, from God Himself, that all of the acts and relationships between God and His creation are acts of the Divine Nature embracing the entire Trinity of Persons. We know, moreover, that our concepts of the words: Father, Son, Holy Spirit, Only Begotten Son, etc., though given us by God Himself, are only analogous terms both in reference to relationships within the Trinity and toward ourselves. They are only the best that can be found within the boundaries of human language, but they fall far short of adequacy to express the marvelous reality.

The same defect applies to the explanations given us by Saint Thomas that the Word is the Eternal Begotten act of the divine Intellect—and that the mutual love willed by the eternal volition of the First and Second Persons brings about the procession of the Third Person. These are only attempts to help us enjoy the effects upon ourselves of the benefits of these relationships,—to help us to see more clearly the preciousness of our status before God, —to help us to understand better the infinite perfection which we know by revelation that God has placed at our disposal.

It helps us to see the connection between the intimate attention to every little detail of our individual lives and the ordering of this limitless universe which we are learning to respect with greater awe the more our ingenuity enables us to penetrate into its depths.

And how does it help us most? It gives us a mental and intellectual frame in which to picture what we know about the blessed Trinity, our God. This frame has its limitations inherent in the gulf between the human and the divine, the natural and the supernatural.

"God the Father" is the symbol given us by Christ

as the First Person. Now, the concept of Father and the concept of First both convey to our minds a connotation of superiority as source or reason for being, a primacy in the realm of being. Indeed, there is nothing in the created world which does not stem from its source as from a cause, at least a secondary cause, of its existence.

So, while the notion of Source and Reason for Being are applicable in a certain sense to the divine Person of God the Father, we must accept the limitation of its application brought to us by the knowledge that the Athanasian Creed teaches us that our salvation depends upon our acceptance of the fact that each of the three Persons is Uncaused, Uncreated, Eternal, Omnipotent—and yet there are not three Uncaused, three Uncreated, three Eternals, three Omnipotents, but One in All and All in One.

And yet the Son does stem from the Father by an eternal process which we are taught by God to call begetting, omitting the limitation which applies to this word in our natural experience. And the Holy Spirit stems from the Father and the Son by an eternal action which we have been taught to call spiration or proceeding.

With this background of knowledge, let us look further into the meaning of our declaration when we say: "I believe in God the Father almighty" in reciting the Creed. Perhaps the most obvious attribute of the Divine Nature which appeals to us as appropriate to assign to God the Father is Power. The most notable thing about God is His power-to-be. It is His power to BE that accounts for everything else that is. The most awesome thing God ever said to man is this: "I am He who IS!"

And coupled with this awesome attribute of power-to-be, is power to create. The manifestation of this power to create is the universe which we see. But by far the greatest item of this manifestation is the fact that *we* see it. In other words, all the rest of creation is explained by the presence of beings capable of knowing and appreciating it. And this ability to appreciate it crowds upon us creatures who have it, the notion that the second attribute most appropriate to God the Father is infinite generosity.

The universe with-us-in-it adds nothing to God's happiness. His happiness was infinitely perfect before the world was made and it will be infinitely perfect throughout eternity at the end of time. No, the only explanation of the universe-with-us-in-it is that God made it for us to enjoy, and He placed us in it that it might be enjoyed.

But God's purpose in creating us does not end with the enjoyment of the universe. In fact, our enjoyment of the universe is only one of the means provided by God to enable us to know Him and love Him and so to share in His happiness.

That is the acme of His generosity. We cannot add to *His* happiness, we can only manifest it by loving *Him*. We cannot add to His glory, we can only manifest it by adoring His generosity. But in this act of loving adoration we enter upon a plane which, by an added act of God's generosity, elevates mankind far above all the rest of the physical universe. It is the supernatural plane of grace whereby man is prepared for spiritual union with God and a share in God's beatific and eternal happiness in heaven.

All this is very abstract and academic and must be brought into focus for the benefit of each one of us here and now in order to make us realize what privileged creatures we are. The first move to establish such a focus involves another item that is appropriately attributed to God the Father. It is: that every tiny event in the history of creation has been planned and willed by the Wisdom of God.

It is true that the Wisdom or Word of the Godhead is the symbol of the Second Person of the Trinity, but it is ordinarily conceived that the Person of the Word is in some way the act of the divinity carrying out the divine plan. This is conveyed by the expression: "by the Father through the Son" or "in the Son". *Per ipsum et cum ipso et in ipso*.

This notion is, moreover, made certain by the Second Person Himself in His humanity. Nothing in the teaching of Christ is more constantly repeated by Him than His insistence that all His acts are in conformity with the will of the Father. His whole life on earth is an enactment of His statement: "Even as the Father hath commanded Me thus I do." (John 14:31). "The Son cannot do anything of Himself but what He sees the Father doing; for whatever He does, this the Son does likewise." (John 5:19). "My food," said Jesus to them, "is to do the will of Him who sent Me, and to accomplish His work." (John 4:34). "I seek not My own will, but the will of Him who sent Me." (John 5:30). "And the word that you hear is not Mine but the word of the Father who sent Me." (John 14:24). It is interesting to note that the word "Sent" as used by Christ in this connection is repeated thirty-eight times in the Gospel of Saint John alone.

This should indeed give us an entirely new and alert insight into the meaning and loving importance of those familiar words of the Lord's Prayer which I finally decided to use as the theme of this chapter. The chief reason for their importance is that they come to us directly from the lips of Christ who is God and who, as we have just seen, declared Himself to be the divine Instrument who came not only to achieve our salvation but to make known to us the majestic plan of God the Father whereby each of us individually may share in that salvation.

Not only does its source make the Lord's Prayer important, but its form bespeaks its Author in every word. It puts our access to God the Father on a new and precious foundation of love rather than fear. It has been very skillfully shown by the late Father Albert Kleber, O.S.B. of Saint Meinrad's Abbey, how Christ, in the Our Father, has mellowed the austere commands of the Decalogue given to Moses under circumstances inspiring fear and trembling, and has given us this same Decalogue in acts of divine homage and petition. (C.B.Q. Vol. III p. 302-320). It is not just *a* prayer, but it is the essence of all prayer and contains all that is to be desired. As Father Albert has put it: "Such a prayer will of necessity be a divinely perfect application of the self-evident principle later worded by Pope Saint Celestine, *'Ut legem credendi lex statuat supplicandi.'* Faith must be the basis of prayer." (Ibid. p. 303).

And not only does this majestic prayer give us a law of faith, but a law of living as well. The first two phrases of the Creed and the first two Commandments of the Decalogue set forth in cold imperative the law of fear, albeit the central truth of revelation upon which all else depends: I believe in God the Father almighty, Creator of heaven and earth. I am the Lord thy God; thou shalt not have strange gods before Me. Thou shalt not take the Name of the Lord thy God in vain.

The first two phrases of the Lord's Prayer take these stern commandments of faith and transmute them into the melody of the law of sonship and love. Our Father who art in heaven hallowed be Thy Name. What wealth of faith, of hope in heaven, of love of God and man is packed into those ten words! Christ taught us to say, not "my Father", not "The

Father", but "Our Father"—made so by Christ's gracious incorporation of all of us as brothers into the inheritance of true sonship to be realized in full by spiritual reunion in heaven.

The loving expression: "Hallowed be Thy Name" contrasts with the Psalmist's "Holy and terrible is His Name." (Ps. 110:9). But, the lesson above all which we should gain from this meditation on God the Father in heaven, is contained in the next two phrases of our text: "Thy kingdom come; Thy will be done on earth as it is in heaven." (Matt. 6:10).

First and foremost, we must learn to know that the Kingdom of God which is constantly unfolding before the eyes of men is the perfect plan embracing every detail in the life of every one of us, even those apparent evils and the trials which we find the hardest to understand. When we say: "Thy Kingdom come" we should learn to mean: Dear God our Father, I believe that everything that happens to me is under Your complete control and is planned by You for my welfare if I accept it in cooperation with the grace which I know You will give me.

That is the true meaning of the coming of the Kingdom of God as it was expressed for us by Christ who is God. And when we say: "Thy will be done," we should always mean: "I accept whatever happens with loving confidence as being from Thy hand and I submit every thought and word and act of mine to what You teach me as Your will."

Christ Himself is our infallible Model in this regard. In Gethsemane His divine nature foresaw all the wicked torture which He was about to face and His human nature recoiled from it in terror and especially was He repelled by the forthcoming perfidy of those He loved the most, not only Judas, but unfaithful priests and people all down the centuries. He begged that if it were possible He might be spared these heartbreaks. But every time He ended His prayer: "Nevertheless, not as I will but as Thou wilt." (Matt. 26:39).

And this same prayer of Christ applies directly to every one of us when we are faced with the greatest trials and hardships of our lives as well as in the ordinary events of every day. Christ told His disciples that it was *necessary* that the Son of Man should suffer these things and enter into His glory. (Luke 24:26). It was necessary only because it was in accordance with His Father's ineffable plan and will. He also told them: "It is necessary that scandals come." (Matt. 18:7). These are all a part of the approach to the kingdom of God which we are being prepared to enter by cooperating with God's grace to do His will on earth in faith and hope that we may one day rejoice with Him in heaven where His will reigns supreme in perfect love.

CHAPTER X

JESUS CHRIST OUR LORD

Having sought a better understanding of the majesty of the Holy Trinity, we are now invited to study further the infinite treasure offered to us by the Incarnation of the Second Person of that Trinity who lives among us now and is ready to save us from the *danger* that surrounds us on every side. He is here to defend us from Satan as truly as when He said to the Samaritan woman at Jacob's well: "If thou hadst known the gift of God, and who He is who is saying to thee, 'Give Me a drink.' Thou wouldst have asked Him and He would have given thee Living Water." (John 4:10). These words should arouse within us a keen desire to respond spiritually as did the Samaritan woman naturally, to that invitation to drink the living water offered to us by Jesus Christ our Lord.

When we recite the Apostles Creed we declare that, by the light of faith, we acknowledge Jesus Christ our Lord as God. Ever since the days the Apostles themselves declared their crucified Leader to be True God, every convert who is admitted into the Church must have received this same supernatural virtue of faith and must have made this same act of faith in the divinity of Jesus Christ.

On the other hand, practically every heresy of the past two thousand years has stemmed from some distortion of the bed-rock simplicity of that declaration of faith. For no denial of the doctrine left by Jesus in the Deposit of Faith is possible if one really knows who He is who put it there.

The explicit denial of His divinity during the early centuries led to a further clarification of our declaration of faith. This was finally crystallized into the equally explicit *affirmation* of His Divinity contained in the Athanasian Creed which, unfortunately, is all too unfamiliar even among Catholics today, and which has been virtually rejected by the Church of England for the very reason that it contains within itself the declaration that salvation depends upon acknowledgement that Jesus Christ is very God.

The Church of England does not consider this a necessary article of faith and has of necessity modified its doctrine in this regard to provide that one may continue to be a member in good standing and even recite the Apostles Creed saying: "I believe . . . in Jesus Christ His only Son our Lord, etc. . . ." and mean "I repeat these symbolic phrases and believe that they are," to use the words of their own Commission on Christian Doctrine, "pictorial expressions of spiritual truths, even though the supposed facts themselves did not actually happen" (*Doetrine in the Church of England*, Macmillan p. 37).

It would, indeed, be hard to accommodate such doctrinal latitude within the following partial quotation from our Athanasian Creed:

> "Whoever would be saved, before all things it is necessary that he hold the Catholic Faith.
>
> Which faith, except every one does keep entire, and unviolated, without doubt he shall perish everlastingly."
>
> Furthermore, "It is necessary to everlasting salvation, that he also believe rightly the Incarnation of our Lord Jesus Christ.
>
> Now, the right faith is that we believe and confess that our Lord Jesus Christ, the Son of God, is both God and Man.
>
> He is God, of the substance of His Father, begotten before the world; and He is Man, of the substance of His Mother, born in the world.
>
> Perfect God, perfect Man: subsisting in a rational soul and human flesh.

Who although He be both God and Man, yet He is not two, but one, Christ."

Now, why is it necessary for any Christian to reject this form of the Creed, and why does any one find it necessary to vitiate the other forms of the Creed by detaching from them the acknowledgement of concomitant historical fact? The answer is quite simple. There is a collection of documents which we call The New Testament which can be and have been identified as the writings of contemporaries of Jesus of Nazareth who were His disciples. These documents contain statements which make it certain that this Man-God, Jesus of Nazareth, chose twelve men whom He taught for nearly three years, giving them a body of truth which they must believe, and a form of worship which they must practice. He constituted them the hierarchy of His Church which He founded on them with Saint Peter as their head and foundation-stone. He then commanded them to teach all men for all time all that He had told them that they must believe and do to be saved.

To make this possible, He gave them supernatural powers, first to perpetuate the sacrificial offering of His Body and Blood as the central act of worship until the end of time; second, to forgive sins when they were confessed with contrition and purpose of amendment. And finally, He clinched the continuity of His Church until the end of time by promising them and their successors the perpetual companionship of His Holy Spirit who would infallibly protect them by divine power from forgetting or changing any of the essentials of doctrine or worship which He had taught them. He also promised them that even the power of hell should never be able to exterminate this One, Holy, Universal Church which they were to perpetuate until the end of time.

Jesus Christ Our Lord

The most deadly feature of the *danger* which we face in the present day is that this very promise of Christ is being denied by the acts and words of some of the false leaders within the Church who, in grave disloyalty to the Holy Father, are seeking to destroy this bed-rock foundation of faith.

But, to return to the answer regarding the Church of England and other Protestant Churches: it is obviously impossible to account for the fact that they teach different doctrine and practice different worship from that taught and practiced by the Church for the first fifteen hundred years of her existence unless it can be shown that the former Church taught false doctrine and practiced false worship. It therefore becomes impossible to maintain with unequivocal certainty that the doctrine was specific, or that the promises were made, or that the supernatural powers were conferred. All of which removes the possibility of declaring with unequivocal certainty that the Man was God who made the promises and taught the doctrine and conferred the powers.

Since, however, that would leave a rather sorry remnant upon which to base one's faith, it is seldom publicly declared and taught that He was not God, but those who wish to believe that He was God are left to find their own answer for the claim that the Church He founded has failed. But equally obviously it cannot be maintained by them that salvation depends upon belief that He is the God-Man who is described in the Athanasian Creed and to whom the words of the Apostles Creed, when used in their ordinary sense, ascribe the nature of God.

Now, why have I made this long digression in writing for those who are not only believing Catholics, but are aspiring to follow a way of perfection that will proclaim the divinity of Jesus Christ to all men? It is because of the fact that very many Anglicans, as well as other non-Catholics, *do* wish to believe that Jesus Christ *is* God. And it is certainly true that far too many Catholics behave as if their reason for believing in Him is no more convincing than that available to those who must admit that He was not able to carry out His promises.

Let me hasten to add, however, that this is not a fault-finding discussion of the matter. Quite the contrary, it is intended to be a fervent invitation to join me in seeking to find a way to realize even a tiny part of the treasure, the infinite treasure, that we have received from almighty God on Christmas Day! It is a treasure that can make us saints, far advanced in the Way of Perfection, if we will only use it in the way God intends that it should be used. I mean the full realization of the power bestowed upon us by the indwelling presence of Jesus Christ in our souls, and in our churches, brought there by the action of His Holy Spirit with His supernatural bestowal of virtues and gifts and their fruits.

In other words, I wish to invite the reader to share with me a growing appreciation of the force of Saint Paul's plea to the Galatians (4:19) "My little children, I am in travail over you afresh, until I can see Christ's image formed in you." Or, as it is beautifully expressed by the late Archbishop of Mexico, Luis Martinez: "If only we knew the gift of God; if only we knew what a marvelous world we carry within our soul! If only we realized the incomparable and divine beauty of the supernatural world!" (*The Sanctifier*, p. 140).

It is our privilege to start where much of the rest of the world leaves off, with a clear and unclouded faith in the divinity of our Lord Jesus Christ. And, having this start, it is my hope that we may have Christ formed in us with an ever more perfect and intimate experimental knowledge of His love, together with a way of life which reflects that intimate kinship with the indwelling Christ.

It is the purpose of our life in this world that Christ be formed in us to give us that supernatural maturity with which we will be equipped to enjoy the perfection of that union in the Beatific Vision in heaven. The Way of Perfection on earth is nothing other than the expert cultivation of our supernatural faculties which develop parallel with our natural faculties and gradually divinize them so that we ultimately do the will of God with the same motive of love as did Christ Himself.

Such a practice of the way of perfection will enable every soul to reflect that presence within him, in accordance with his state, as other Christs. This expression is commonly used especially as regards those who, through the Sacrament of Orders, share in and dispense the priestly powers of Christ. But it need by no means be confined to the priestly state as is exemplified in a supreme degree by Our Lady whose body was as intimately united to the natural Christ as was her soul to the divine Christ.

And she, as our Mother in Christ, has passed this capacity on to all of her children so that each of us may learn to say truly, as did Saint Paul: "I live—yet no longer I, but Christ lives in me; and the life I now live in the flesh I live in the faith of the Son of God who loved me and gave Himself up for me." (Gal. 2:20).

And how does it come about that this image of Christ which was so anxiously desired by Saint Paul and which I also desire for you and for myself, may be formed in us? Well, just as we are told in Scripture that Christ's humanity was formed in the Virgin Mother by the power of the Holy Spirit, so also it may be that the spiritual possession of Christ may be formed in her and in us by the power of the Holy

Spirit indwelling in all those who are in a state of Sanctifying Grace.

First of all, however, it requires deep and abiding faith. Faith, by its very nature, is obscure. But the more obscure it is, the more meritorious is wholehearted acceptance of the truth as soon as we are assured that it is guaranteed by God. Here again, the Blessed Virgin was acknowledged as the outstanding example by her cousin Elizabeth: "And blessed art thou who hast believed, for the message of the Lord shall be fulfilled." (Luke 1:45).

And so it is with us. Christ begs us to believe, but He never will coerce our free-will. He said to Saint Thomas: "Blessed are they who have not seen and yet have believed." (John 20:29) Many of the disciples "went away and walked with Him no more" (John 6:66), as Saint John tells us when He said to them: "He who eats My Flesh and drinks My Blood possesses everlasting life". (John 6:54). He had asked them to believe this upon the authority of His statement that it was the will of His Father who had sent Him. When they refused belief He did not detain them, but turned to His Apostles and said: "'Do you also wish to go away?' Simon Peter answered Him, 'Lord, to whom should we go? Thou hast the words of eternal life, and we ourselves steadfastly believe and know that Thou art the Holy One of God'". (John 6:68-69).

And the situation is precisely the same with us today! The Holy Spirit of Christ comes into our souls together with His virtues and gifts, at Baptism or whenever we gain Sanctifying Grace. In an infant the function of these supernatural faculties is nascent just as the function of his natural faculties of intellect and memory and will is nascent. They grow and develop together as the child receives his education. Both are built up on the foundation of faith: Human faith for the natural faculties, divine faith for the supernatural faculties. That is why education without religion is wholly inadequate. And that is why the most grave obligation of parents is to see to the firm foundation of faith in their children as well as in themselves. And this is of great importance in these post-conciliar years since Satan has contrived to distort the true faith in some of the catechisms taught to children even in our "Catholic" schools.

It is only on the foundation of submissive bedrock faith that the supernatural faculties, under the power of the Holy Spirit will build Sanctifying Grace into the true formation of Christ in the soul. It is only through this formation of Christ in us by the Holy Spirit that the true purpose of our life in this world can be accomplished. It is the perfect formation of Christ in us, resulting in perfect union of our will with the will of Christ, that is the sole objective of the Way of Perfection which we are invited to follow.

And what can we do about it? First and foremost, we must learn to depend upon Jesus Christ our Lord. Christ will never coerce our will, but how patiently and powerfully He will *aid our will to believe Him!* In fact, if we will admit our nothingness before Him, He will do it all. His abiding Spirit will build the living Christ into union with our will in proporton to our effort to show Him our love and gratitude.

Now please give me your careful attention! Suppose some supernatural vision were suddenly to enable you to perceive with your bodily senses the glorious Body of Christ offering you His Sacred Heart to unite with your own. Do you suppose that while that vision lasted, it would be possible for you to make yourself guilty of sin—any sin—even the slightest venial sin? You know the answer!

All you have to do to gain that same protection of grace for yourself is to cultivate the help of the Holy Spirit to build an appreciation of that presence of Christ which is a reality in your soul. And that help is cultivated by positive acts on your part. Faith itself, the essential foundation of love, is perfected by working at it, by constant advertence to the necessity of belief, by constant attention to the supernatural helps that are always available to us.

God knows, in these days, the external pressure is all the other way. Satan loses no opportunity to crowd our newspapers, our magazines, our radio and television, with the heresies of materialism and false science which tend to benumb that formation of Jesus Christ within us. It is for us to cultivate those supernatural faculties which start with the unequivocal bedrock faith with which we have been blessed by the infallible doctrine of the Athanasian Creed. These will carry us by means of the Gifts of the Holy Spirit far beyond the intellectual limitations of faith and will teach us by experience to know how to use that priceless treasure which Jesus Christ our Lord has placed at our disposal—His own Sacred Heart.

He is within us ready to inundate our souls with an everlasting fountain of living water, able to quench forever all the fiery darts of the evil one. Then will it come about that our love of His Heart will pervade our every thought and word and act and again we will be brought to see as clearly as did the Apostle Saint Thomas and, falling to our knees we will repeat with him: "My Lord and my God: My God and my All!" (John 20:28)

In conclusion, let us remember this: Our full appreciation of the possession of Christ within us is not going to change the succession of events that will affect our lives from without. It can, however, and will, completely change for us the effect of those events within our hearts and that is what is all-important.

Never in this life can our appreciation of this indwelling presence of Christ be perfect. Never in this life can our faith be free from imperfection. Never in this life can our experiences be free from pain. But all three of these imperfections are willed by God for our eternal welfare and so they can be perfectly accepted for love. It is that which constitutes the Way of Perfection. Pain may take many forms. Perhaps the hardest pain to bear is that mental pain which comes from the words and acts of those we love the most, or the acts of those whom we are obliged to obey. Even that can be a source of joy if it is accepted as an act of love for Jesus Christ who did just that for us!

CHAPTER XI

FACE DANGER WITH MARY

Perhaps the most detestable item of false renewal which has emerged since the Second Vatican Council has been to scale down devotion to the Mother of God. Mary is the one member of the human race chosen by God to be closest to Him in the precious drama of love which He planned to tear down the bondage of Satan and restore mankind to the heritage of love for which He had made the world. Those who are bent on destruction within the Church well know that she is their archenemy and strive to eliminate her as a source of fortitude to those of us who strive against them to meet the *danger* they are causing.

The first Mother of the human race had, by her disobedience, shared in the rebellion which separated all men from God. The all-but-unbelievable means chosen by God to repair the tragedy of that rebellion was that He should take human nature Himself.

But how could God-Man enter into the realm of our sense knowledge when every single candidate for parenthood was under the bondage of Satan and so utterly unfit to usher a Child-God into the world? Only the infinite ingenuity of God and the infinite power of God and the infinite love of the Triune God could provide an answer. This He did by anticipating the saving power which His humanity would provide, to create just one perfect flower to be His Mother to unite His divinity to the human race by a channel utterly suitable to the majesty of God.

To be thus qualified, not only must she be perfect from the moment of the creation of her soul in the womb of her mother, but she must also be wonderfully supplied by almighty God with a plenitude of supernatural grace which would *keep* her perfect in body and soul throughout her life and into eternity. The Blessed Virgin Mary was, then, in being chosen to give Humanity to His Divinity, in the very truest sense, the Handmaid of the Lord; His cooperator, not only to give Him His Humanity, but, all life long, to be the one already perfect helper chosen to unite Him to the object of His redeeming mission.

She was thus made perfect before the Perfector arrived to begin His work; perfect in body and soul, perfect in humility, perfect in obedience, perfect in love which united God to man and which drew all men to God. No wonder that God loved her and gave her all those gifts which kept her incomparably more lovable than any other human being that ever lived or ever will live in the world.

And so she still is; the Mother of divine love, the spiritual Mother bequeathed by God to all men, especially those who have received the spiritual rebirth of Baptism. Immaculately conceived, immaculately preserved from sin all life long, immaculately assumed into heaven where, on a throne at the right hand of Jesus Christ in glory, she still and always intercedes for each one of us with a mother's love made perfect by divine grace. Yes, Mary is still the Handmaid of the Lord to help Him bring to perfection the Church which He has chosen to be the vehicle of His love. And, as His Handmaid, it is her privilege to have a close relationship to Him in His interest for the welfare of every individual soul in the world.

I am particularly sensitive on this point because, like all Protestants, I was very much aloof from and unappreciative of the love Our Lady had for me. And so it is with special love and humility that I acknowledge my debt to her for helping me to see the truth. It is indicative of her intercession in my behalf that

I began my Novitiate on the Feast of her Assumption; I made my monastic profession on that same feast day; and I was ordained to the Holy Priesthood on that same feast day. Naturally, my ordination card shown on the dedication page of this book, was a picture of the Blessed Virgin with arms spread over the world, with the legend: *"Sub Tuum Praesidium"*, Under Thy Protection.

It is most important at this particular time that each one of us should renew our understanding and appreciation of this precious relationship with which God has chosen to enrich the world. This relationship is joyfully and whimsically referred to by one of the busy professional correspondents of Father Thomas V. Moore and quoted by him in his book, *The Life of Man With God*. She says: "I have a great personal friend in our Blessed Mother. I talk to her as I would to my own earthly mother. It is only because of our dear Mother that I am what I am today and she knows that I give her all the credit. She never refuses me anything that is for my good; even finds me parking places when it would seem impossible to most people. The *Memorare* to me is one of the most powerful prayers we have. Thanks, Dear Mother."

After this quotation, I can hardly leave unsaid some comment on the views expressed in a Catholic magazine which the reader may have seen. It is distressing to know that such an article exists but a small sample will suffice to show the disloyalty to the Blessed Virgin that should be opposed. The author says: "The very last thing we should do is to ask Mary for her "intercession".... The whole concept of "intercession" seems an unfortunate hangover from another era . . . it is humiliating to think that the Church could ever have toyed with such things."

I would prefer, however, to quote from the Second

Face Danger With Mary

Vatican Council to help you see the *danger* in postconciliar renewal among the hosts of modern Protestantizers. And I quote:

". . . For, taken up to heaven, she did not lay aside this saving role, but by her manifold acts of intercession continues to win for us gifts of eternal salvation.

"By her maternal charity, Mary cares for the brethren of her Son who still journey on earth surrounded by dangers and difficulties, until they are led to their happy fatherland. Therefore the Blessed Virgin is invoked by the Church under the titles of Advocate, Auxiliatrix, Adjutrix, and Mediatrix."

Our spiritual Mother has indeed been chosen to cement our union with God, but her love also reaches out to those millions from whom that love has been obscured for centuries by a strange denial of her mission given by Christ her Son. This obscurity is doubly tragic as a possible contamination of the atmosphere of dialogue between the Catholic Church and the world at large which was fanned into fervor by the charity of our beloved Holy Father of happy memory, Pope John XXIII, and has been crystalized into form by the constant inspiration of the Holy Spirit made evident in the action of Pope Paul VI until his death, and after him by Pope John Paul I and Pope John Paul II.

To meet this challenge, each one of us should review our attachment to the Blessed Mother of God and be made aware of her part in our individual lives. This is important because our part in the dialogue is chiefly one of prayer and *example* and cordial love of neighbor, and all that is wrapped up in our own individual Project Sainthood.

The *danger* of dim faith and resulting evil example is manifest in the slighting of the Blessed Virgin that false dialogue has produced. It is far better to heed the title of this chapter and Face *Danger* With Mary. This is not because we may have chosen her as our special Patroness but because Christ has chosen her to be the gracious Mother of Divine Grace which is essential for the success of every individual Project Sainthood.

And after all, Christ's infinite love brings it about that the dialogue between His Church and the world is not a mass-attack upon souls with a barrage of grace; it is rather the intimate moulding of Divine Providence utilizing every item of apostolic dialogue to effect the promotion of Project Sainthood in every individual soul in the Church and in the world.

At first thought, it might seem a far cry from the dialogue between the Church and the world, to the part played by the Blessed Mother in our individual Project Sainthood. But a second thought should help us to see that it is of the essence of the dialogue of charity which our Holy Father proposes to us Catholics to present to those who are separated from us.

Saint Paul has given us a very concise statement of the purpose of God in the creation of the world. In his exhortation to the Thessalonians to prepare them for the final judgment, Saint Paul ends his plea thus: ". . . as you have learned from us how you ought to live in pleasing God—just as indeed you do live—so you would progress still more. . . . For this is the will of God—your sanctification." (I. Thes. 4:1-3). In other words, Project Sainthood is the primary purpose for which God has given us life. And, just as God has made it Mary's business to be concerned with Project Sainthood for each one of us, so has He made it Mary's business to be concerned with Project Sainthood for everyone who has not yet become fully united with Christ in His one Sheepfold.

And the reason that this is doubly important to us

to understand at this time is that this is one point of doctrine in which those who may be the sharers of our dialogue emphatically agree with us, but most unfortunately they are emphatically unaware that this is so! For surely, no one in the world, not even one who professes atheism, would deny that sanctification, in the sense that we give it, or eternal perfect happiness, would be most welcome to him. He therefore definitely agrees with us that our version of the end for which man is created is indeed to be desired, *if true!*

Mankind, therefore, agrees with us that each individual Project Sainthood is something to be desired and cultivated. It is, then, for us to show mankind that his agreement on this point involves agreement regarding the necessity of his interest in the love of Our Lady because grace is a necessity for sainthood and God has made Our Lady a loving dispenser of His grace, not by any choice of ours but because it is fitting in His eyes that she should be.

The only reason that mankind is unaware of this truth which has been taught and practiced by the Church ever since it was given to us by Christ, is that Our Lady's intimacy with the Redeeming Sacrifice of Christ made her be set aside when the continuity of that Sacrifice was denied by those who have separated themselves from the sacrificial worship of the Church. It is worthy of attention that this devoted love of Mary does still persist among all of those who are still fed by this Sacramental Sacrifice in the Oriental Church, even though they have forsaken their loyalty to the Church founded by Christ upon Saint Peter. It is by the intercession of Our Lady-of-the-atonement, that these will be made one with us once more. Just so, it is her love and her intercession that must appear in the dialogue with those who have lost sight of the fact or have never known that grace comes to them through her.

So, let us recall the urgent wish of our late Holy Father, Pope Paul, which he recommended to the Council and which the Council wholeheartedly supported, that the dialogue with which Christ's Catholic Church enters the present Ecumenical Movement of the world has for its first objective to show our non-Catholic Christian brothers how much of their belief agrees with Catholic doctrine. Let us also recall the warning of Pope John Paul II, as of all the Popes who have preceded him, that we should detest and shun the notion of watering-down the doctrine of the Deposit of Faith to make it fit with the present teaching of those with whom we hope to establish our dialogue.

Admittedly, there is a great temptation to do just that. The root of this temptation is the notion held by almost all of those with whom we wish to establish dialogue, that our doctrine, like theirs, is merely our interpretation of Scripture and tradition, arrived at perhaps with prayer and careful study but nonetheless a product of reason. The logical and normal reaction, when this notion is brought to bear upon our incapacity to whittle down doctrine, is to regard it as stubborn and prideful intransigence that simply repels further dialogue. Or, as it was expressed in a letter to me from a devout Christian lady which I have quoted before: "The unbending attitude of being completely right and brooking no disagreement with its teachings is intolerance of the worst kind and far from a Christian attitude."

The reason for such a response is characteristic and fundamental. It is of a piece with *being* a non-Catholic. It unfortunately expresses annoyance and hostility, not so much because of the particular matter of the difference, but because of being unaware of the reason for the difference of doctrine. The non-

Face Danger With Mary

Catholic is usually almost totally unaware of the Catholic *motive* for faith. With the Catholic, it is not at all a question of "brooking no disagreement with the teaching"—it is not a *question* of agreement or disagreement—it is solely a question of: "Is this the teaching that Christ gave to the Apostles to hand down to me in accordance with His command and His promise of protection from error?"

In other words, it is not a question of—"Do I agree with the doctrine?" but—"Is it the word of God?" If it is the word of God, disagreement vanishes and is replaced by adoration of the love which provides the protection from error. To the Catholic, if it were not the word of God, his faith would be nonsense and the world a sham, all of which is impossible because there is too much evidence to the contrary—chief of which is that none of the teaching ever *has* been changed since Christ gave it to the Apostles.

And that brings up the true reason for resisting the temptation to water-down the doctrine, especially when there is question of doctrine respecting Our Lady, which is perhaps most frequently an obstacle to dialogue. The fact that the love of Catholics for Our Lady does constitute an obstacle to dialogue, has caused many of those who call themselves liberals and who wish to pit their judgment against that of our Popes, to rashly advocate that we should "soft-pedal" and down-grade the doctrine of Mary's place in the divine economy.

One of the most venomous forms of this downgrading of Our Lady is the insinuation of the uncertainty of the apparitions which have formed the basis of the devotions at the great Marian shrines such as Lourdes, Fatima, and Guadalupe. It is sometimes asserted that Catholics may casually disregard the genuineness of these apparitions because they are not authenticated by the solemn definition of the infallible Teaching Authority of the Church. The evil of such an assertion lies in the insinuation that the entire matter is subject to doubt and may be safely ignored by Catholics.

It is perfectly true that such matters cannot be made the subjects of solemn definition for the very reason that solemn definition, in accordance with God's promise, is limited to items of public revelation dating from Apostolic times. Throughout the history of the Church, however, the unmistakable evidence of divine assistance has helped to mould the body of doctrine and bring it into focus on a far wider scale than the bare bones of infallible declarations. To intimate that the Church's acceptance and approval of this evidence without using infallible decrees, leaves Catholics without certain knowledge of the authenticity of the apparitions and the devotions at such shrines as Lourdes, Fatima, and Guadalupe is, to put it mildly, rash temerity in the extreme.

And in this same vein, Mary's plea for the Rosary as a weapon against Communism, has been talked-down instead of being boosted. My answer to that is to carry the biggest Rosary I can find and pray fifteen decades every day!

This is all most important at this particular time when the example of Catholic thought and behavior is being scrutinized with honest perceptive attention by more non-Catholics than at any previous time in the history of the Church. It is indeed true that veneration of the Blessed Virgin is regarded as idolatry by very many non-Catholic Christians. But what a colossal mistake it would be to invite them into dialogue which would insinuate that Catholic doctrine could be accommodated to their views in this regard.

It would be a grave injustice to them, to Our Lady, and to us, to down-grade her importance in order

Face Danger With Mary

to promote this dialogue. God has made it abundantly clear during recent centuries that the choice of Mary to be His Mother and the Mother of those whom He has made His brothers, and the Mother of His Church, is to be an ever-increasing invitation to all men to share in her love, her intercession and His love. He is constantly up-grading the evidence of His wish to have us come to Him through her gracious assistance.

This evidence has been given a tremendous boost of hope by the emergence of the *Marian Movement of Priests* which has come into being as a result of words of Our Lady reported in the book: *Our Lady Speaks to Her Beloved Priests*. It is true that it stems from private revelation made by Our Lady to an obscure Italian priest, Don Stefano Gobbi. It began when he was at Fatima on May 8, 1972. Our Lady told Him that she was about to form an army of priests consecrated to her Immaculate Heart, which was to be called *"The Marian Movement of Priests."*

Since that first communication, Father Gobbi has reported the words of Our Lady to her Beloved Priests at intervals which, in the fifth English edition, extend to May 13, 1979 and cover approximately 280 pages.

The objective of this *Marian Movement of Priests* is to summon priests who will unite in an army to be trained by Our Lady to meet the growing number of apostate priests who remain in the Church and spread disloyalty to the Holy Father and the Magisterium. The following excerpts from the book will give an idea of its contents:

> "At the Cenacle, there were the Apostles with Mary, the Mother of Jesus. . . . I wish to bring together the priests of my Movement with Mary, the Mother of Jesus, who is particularly their Mother.

Why do I want them gathered at the Cenacle with me?

— *To Stay With Me,* so that I can nourish and form them myself, and cause them to grow in the perfect consecration to me; so that they may be uniquely my priests and that in them and through them, I may manifest myself anew.

— *To Pray With Me.* When my priests are united among themselves and with me in prayer, how efficacious their prayer is! For then, it is I myself who, in them, accomplishes my task of eternal intercession to God for all my children. Let them be united among themselves and with me during the celebration of Holy Mass, in the recitation of the Liturgy of the Hours, in praying the Rosary—this prayer which is mine. The Rosary is the weapon that I give myself to these priests, my sons, to fight against the approaching great struggles that await them.

— *To Love One Another* and to live in a true fraternity in the company of their Mother. Today it is necessary that my priests know each other, that they be like brothers assembled by their Mother around her. There is too much solitude, there is too much abandonment for my priest-sons today. I do not want them to be alone: let them help one another, let them feel and really be all brothers to one another.

— *To Wait* for the decisive moments that are approaching closer and closer. The time is near when some poor priests, my sons, will come out in the open to set themselves against my Son, against me, against the Church and against the Gospel. Then the cohort of my priests, prepared and led by me, will have to come forth into the open to proclaim, with courage and before everyone, the divinity of my Son, the reality of all my privileges, the necessity of the hierarchical Church united to the Pope and under his authority, and all the truths contained in the Gospel. Many priests, wavering and almost overcome by the tempest, will follow your example and return to the road of salvation."

Face Danger With Mary

That this call to priests is being answered is shown by the fact that it has been translated into all major languages and in the United States the fifth printing, of one-hundred-thousand copies is ready for distribution. A letter of March 12, 1979 from the United States Headquarters reports that more than twenty-thousand priests have become members in the six years of its existence.

This Movement is also of interest to lay people and Religious who are invited to make a similar Act of Consecration to the Immaculate Heart of Mary as Associates of the Marian Movement of Priests.

> NOTE: Copies of the book: *Our Lady Speaks to Her Beloved Priests*, can be obtained by sending a donation to *The Marian Movement of Priests* (in U.S.A.) c/o Rev. Albert G. Roux, Saint Charles Rectory, P. O. Box 8, Saint Francis, Maine 04774. (in Canada) c/o Rev. Philippe Roy, C.P. 294, Limoilou, Quebec, Canada G1L 4V8.

And so, to return to our consideration of devotion to the Mother of God in connection with our dialogue with non-Catholic Christians: Christ has taught us from the Cross that Mary is the Mediatrix of the graces that He has won for us. This, however, should not be understood in the sense that disturbs many non-Catholics, that is placing her *between* us and Himself and so withdrawing Himself from us. No! it is not her prerogative to exercise any power of her own in bestowing grace other than the power of loving intercession, but it is just that which makes Him so much the more available to us. He is the sole provider of grace; His Passion is the sole source of Redemption; His Church is the sole vehicle of Salvation bringing us His Sacrifice and the Sacraments which He has provided for us. But that by no means minimizes the importance of her function as His coadjutrix through whom all of these treasures come to us, not by courtesy, not by imagination, not by ritual, but directly because God has so ordered it in accordance with His infinite wisdom.

Many analogies have been drawn for us to clarify this office of Our Lady as Mediatrix of graces. The one I like best has been suggested by Our Lord Himself. It is to think of the treasures of our faith as coming to us as spiritual food served at a great banquet to which we are all invited. Christ, the Royal Owner and Provider of it all, sits at the head of the table and by His power keeps it supplied with everything we have need of. But Our Mother Mary is the loving hostess to whom we pass our plates while she heaps them high with more than we ever dare to ask for. How this analogy lends itself to our everyday human experience! For who would deny that access to the heart of a great and generous person is most effectively won through the gentle intercession of his Mother?

The prayer used by the Legion of Mary in their *Catena Legionis*, after the recitation of the Magnificat, expresses this relationship admirably: "O Lord Jesus Christ Our Mediator with the Father, who hast been pleased to appoint the most Blessed Virgin, Thy Mother, to be our Mother also, and our Mediatrix with Thee, mercifully grant that whosoever comes to Thee seeking Thy favors may rejoice to receive them all through Her. Amen."

Far from being an intruder between Christ and the children of His Church, it is the humility of Mary's love that unites us to Him and to her. And far from assuming to herself the prestige that her superlative goodness has earned for her, she relates it all in loving confidence to her Divine Son just as she did when she introduced His Divinity to the world at the marriage feast at Cana. It was by her intercession that Jesus worked His first public miracle, but her example to the beneficiaries of that miracle was an expression of docility to the will of Christ when she said: "Whatever He bids you, do it." (John 2:5).

The corporate dialogue of the Church to the world has been planned by the Council and will be executed under the direction of ecclesiastical authority, but we as individuals can do much to influence its success in accord with the urgent invitation of our late Holy Father Pope Paul VI, who invites us with these words: "We bless and encourage all those who, under the guidance of competent authority, take part in the life giving dialogue of the Church, priests especially and religious, and our well loved laity, dedicated to Christ in Catholic action and in so many other associations and activities." (*Eccl. Suam*, p. 39)

We can begin immediately to do our part by exhibiting that *example* of docile confidence in authority and that ardent love of our neighbor both within and without the Fold, that will lead them all to see the treasure offered by Christ. Thus we will win by example a better support from Catholics; and by love, the confidence of non-Catholics to see it as an offering of love and not as an "unbending attitude of being completely right" as so many non-Catholics affirm.

When Mary said to the Angel Gabriel: "Behold the Handmaid of the Lord, be it done to me according to Thy word!" (Luke 1:38) she made herself not only the Mother but the loving partner of each one of us in carrying the love of her Divine Son to all those who are not now aware of His love or hers. Reunion or conversion would be impossible without grace. Mary presides at the banquet of grace. Let us do our part to help her invite those who are still strangers to her love. Project Sainthood for us and for each of them is indeed Mary's business!

CHAPTER XII

DANGER AND VOCATIONS

Some time ago I was called upon to address the Serra Club in Pasadena, California. Naturally, the gist of my talk to the Serrans related to the promotion of vocations to the Priesthood. Taken by itself, that would not be altogether appropriate for our discussion of the *danger* faced by all of us from the decay of Supernatural Faith within the Church and the wholesale example of evil that has resulted. But, since I gave that talk, the bad example given by all too many priests and parents and the pitiful dearth of vocations as a result of that example has made it a major item of *danger* that must be faced by all of us. And each one of us has a grave responsibility to do something about it.

The imposition of a modern equivalent of the Oath Against Modernism to be renewed at intervals by all priests and some provision to enable Bishops to have better control over the behavior of their priests, is in grave need of support all over the world. Of course, local problems differ, but everywhere the great majority of holy and loyal priests is gravely hampered by the evil broadcast by those who are disloyal to their vocation.

There is little question but that this is one of the crucial times in the history of the Church. That does not mean however, that we should be discouraged. It does mean that we should be prepared to stand up and be counted among those who trust God one hundred per cent and reject with scorn the counsel of those who take it upon themselves to broadcast patronizing contempt of the age-long teaching of the Church and grave disloyalty to our Holy Father.

It seems incredible that men who have given

enough evidence of understanding Catholic Faith to be judged worthy of receiving the Sacrament of Holy Orders, should be oblivious of its one essential characteristic. But it is equally impossible to reconcile their words and their behavior with the knowledge that God The Holy Spirit really does fulfill the promises of Christ guaranteeing the integrity of our Faith.

The doubt cast upon this integrity of Faith by the blatant reporting in the secular press of the deviation of many of our priests and people from the perennial teaching of our Magisterium is directly responsible for the pitiful dearth of vocations and departures from the priesthood in our day.

One of my confreres at Westminster Abbey recently attended a Vocation Work-Shop in the city of Vancouver, British Columbia. It was attended by priests and Religious and parents of Catholic young people as well as by representative members of the groups from which vocations might be expected to come.

The discussions at the meeting seemed to disclose the very opposite of enthusiastic encouragement toward vocations. Speeches made by the young people themselves as well as those made by their parents, seemed almost unanimous in declaring that the priesthood and the life of the vocation of a Religious have been so hampered by the restrictions imposed by the out-of-date hierarchy that they are no longer relevant to the needs of the modern Church.

It was argued that practically all the functions performed by priests and Religious could be carried out much more effectively by people who were not subject to absentee authoritarian domination by those who are out of touch with the needs of our day.

The long-term commitment of the priesthood and the life of Religious was also posited as an antiquated obstruction to individual versatility in adapting one's own talents to social needs. The notion of obedience to a prescribed code of behavior also came in for its share of ridicule.

Even among the priests present, a vocation was spoken of as "one of many ways of doing good."

Now, all this travesty of the very meaning of the word "vocation" is symptomatic of the world-wide cult of material science; devotion to the natural; exaltation of the findings of our senses—and oblivion of the all-important power that keeps it all in being and is revealed to us only if we are willing to take God's word for it.

There is one all-inclusive difference between a vocation to the priesthood or the Religious life and any other vocation for men or women. That difference is one hundred per cent invisible, unmeasurable, and therefore unintelligible to the purely natural minded man, be he priest or teen-ager or lay man or woman in any walk of life.

The Triune God is the one *intrinsic* reality and He is one hundred per cent supernatural. All that is natural is the transitory manifestation of the One who keeps it all in being. Everything that God has made is good. God has even told us that it is all *very* good. But all of it is merely the setting in which God's purpose of creation is carried out.

This natural setting is indeed a necessary vehicle for the achievement of God's purpose, but it is only incidental to the supernatural end for which He has created the world. It is the supernatural function of the priest and the Religious working in the natural setting that makes it the most precious vocation that can be given by God to men. Their doings may take every form of good works, both corporal and spiritual, but their value lies in their purpose in God's plan to bring souls to heaven in the end.

To view the priesthood as merely "one of the many

ways of doing good" is to miss entirely the real reason for its preciousness. For a priest to view his own vocation in that light, is to admit the absence of supernatural insight and to place him among those who are candidates for the devastating deception with which Satan is fortifying the "Gates of Hell".

The tragedy of it is that the scandal given by these priests and the lay people who are misled by them goes far beyond their immediate milieu due to their exploitation in the secular press and even most pitifully in the so-called "Catholic" press. It is no wonder that our young people are daunted and led to discount the true mission of the priesthood which we can only know by taking God's word for it.

The situation is doubly serious at the present time because the obvious shortage of vocations and the defections among the priesthood are themselves the greatest dampeners of the supernatural appraisal of the Sacrament of Holy Orders.

God has made it very clear that the Magisterium of the Church, with its authority to teach, govern and sanctify, is an instrument of His creation endowed with supernatural powers to bring men to heaven. It is commanded and fortified by God to be the instrument of the prolongation of God's own life upon earth.

Each one of us can do much to promote a return to the true motive for vocations by insisting on the unchanging supernatural nature of our Faith in our own families and in all our contacts however far they may extend. God has imposed upon Himself a limitation in that He insists that He be brought to us through the ministration of priests who are mortal men who are as frail as other men. But God has also given us the guarantee that these men, frail as they may be, are protected by His Holy Spirit so that they may carry out His will. Beyond that, God leaves it to us to choose.

Forty-five years ago when I left the Protestant Episcopal Church to become a Catholic, a prediction of the behavior of the dissenters within the Church such as we have today, would have been tossed aside as utterly preposterous and unbelievable. It is still unbelievable as to right thinking, but it is here and God allows it as He always has allowed such things because He insists that souls must do their own choosing. He has given all the evidence that is needed to teach us that He will people heaven with those who will take their stand on His invisible and supernatural dominion over all that is. And that is all that the Catholic Church has to offer to any one within or without the Fold.

The present turmoil within the Church has resulted from an unbelievable defection from a supernatural trust in God and a Protestantizing adherence to the purely natural private opinion of "Tom, Dick and Harry" on a basis of natural appeal. And I want none of it!

The Mystical Body of Christ is still the same as it has always been because it is managed by Almighty God. That being true, each one of us can do the most to promote vocations by becoming apostles of The-Church-Guided-By-The-Holy-Spirit and manifest in the Holy See—as distinguished from The-Church-Deformed-By-The-Vote-Of-The-Dissenters and reported by the secular press.

There is not one clause in the Documents of the Second Vatican Council or in the pronouncements of any of the popes since Pope John XXIII that justifies the welter of misinterpretation and the broadcasting of private opinion that is going on today.

Our Faith is not, and never has been, a consensus arrived at by taking a vote as to the precepts of men.

It *is*, and always has been a *one hundred per cent supernaturally guarded revelation of God's will*. There is no thought that I could propose to the reader that has a greater chance of reviving vocations to the priesthood and the Religious life than the broadcasting of this evidence of Divine Love.

What I am suggesting is by no means easy. It may seem to be futile in view of the overwhelming pressure of the pagan notions of materialism which surround us. The Christopher motto, however, is eminently needed here and now "It is better to light one candle than to curse the darkness." Each one of us can lead the way in an ever-widening circle of devotion to our Faith and the means of its propagation which has been devised by God.

This is by no means an occasion for discouragement but it is an occasion for resolution and a renewal of our awareness of the utter adequacy of God to meet every emergency caused by the vagaries of fallen man. The power available to us is guaranteed by the promises of Christ and is not weakened by the defections that have occurred. It is, in fact, made more necessary and more powerful for those who stick to the Faith as God has made it known to us.

I am writing this chapter on the Feast of the Baptism of Our Lord Jesus Christ which commemorates the events chosen by God to expand the revelation initiated by His call to Abraham and up to that time confined to His Chosen People. It was the Epiphany and the Baptism of Christ that God had chosen to manifest the fulfillment of His revelation that the precious Faith He had given to Israel was to be extended to all men. It is proclaimed in the Second Lesson of the Feast of the Baptism of Jesus in these words of Saint Peter:

"The truth I have come to realize, is that God does not have favorites, but that anybody of any nationality who fears God and does what is right is acceptable to Him. It is true that God sent His word to the people of Israel and it was to them that the good news was brought by Jesus Christ but Jesus Christ is Lord of all men." (Acts 10:34–36).

What a wholesome source of vocations would emerge if the Jewish people of today were given the grace to consider these words of their courageous compatriot, Saint Peter! It could bring to this present day a glorious flowering of the precious Faith which God long ago gave to their Nation to lead all men to the goal for which God made the world.

Oh! what a potent invitation there is for the Jewish people of today to recognize two thousand years of added proof of the Resurrection of *their* Savior.

If they would admit the evil that was done to them, with what joy Christ would welcome His Jewish brethren back as the wellspring of His present "Chosen People". How it would demolish the evil now being perpetrated by the Communists and Atheists and false priests, if the Jews would flock back into faithfulness to Christ their Redeemer to share in His Body and Blood and His Sacrifice for them!

This generation is poised on the crest of a wave that will crash into a chaos that would make the trials of the 1930's sound like play-time *or* enter a millenium of peace under Christ that would unite all men in justice, truth and love. The Jewish People could swing the balance *if* they would accept *their Christ*.

It is appalling to realize the lost opportunity for national grandeur which slipped from the hands of Israel when the Sanhedrin failed to recognize the folly of denying the Resurrection of Jesus Christ which had been made certainly known to them by

Danger and Vocations

their own guards at the tomb. Gamaliel seemed to be the only member of the Sanhedrin who sensed the monstrous folly of denying the evidence furnished by God that the Resurrection had occurred and that it proved beyond a doubt that Jesus was their promised Savior.

Of course, each event in the early history of Christianity occurred exactly as it was willed by God whose infinite wisdom used the thoughts and words of men to bring about the acts which perfected His plan.

Instead of allowing Gamaliel's keen insight to bestow this treasure upon the Israel of the First Century, God used it to defer the execution of Peter and the apostles until they had fulfilled all that He had planned for them. The following words from the Acts of the Apostles show the neatness of God's use of Gamaliel's insight to prevent the disaster which threatened His plans:

> "Peter and the apostles said in reply (to the High Priest): 'We must obey God rather than men. The God of our fathers raised up Jesus, whom you murdered by hanging Him on a tree. Him has God exalted with His own right hand to be Prince and Savior, to give repentance to Israel and forgiveness of sins. And we are witnesses of these facts; . . .'"

> "Now when they heard this they became infuriated, and were minded to have them executed. But a Pharisee named Gamaliel, a doctor of the law, and highly respected by all the people, stood up in the Council and directed that the men be taken out for a short time. Then he said to them: 'Men of Israel, be cautious how you propose to act with regard to these men. . . . I say to you, stand aloof from these men, and let them alone. Because if this design or movement be from men it will be wrecked; but if it is from God, you will not be able to put them down; and perhaps you may even find yourselves in conflict with God.'" (cf. Acts 5:28–39).

And for nineteen centuries God has given amazing proof that neither Judaism nor Christianity is "from men" and so neither has been wrecked even against bitter and constant persecution. No persecution has been able to put either of them down. And so, we may take Gamaliel's word for it that both are "from God."

But the nineteen centuries of survival give added proof that the Resurrection identifies the Church founded by Jesus Christ as the ultimate vehicle of salvation. However, the immensely enlarged power and influence of Judaism as of today make it hard to see how anything other than union of the two great religions of the One God could fulfill His plan.

Could it be that God, forseeing the tremendous power that Satan is gaining in the present day, has waited until now to bring to the hearts of Christians and Jews the startling way in which Gamaliel's caution to the Jews has proved beyond doubt that both are equally "of God"? Could it be that both now are invited to unite against the Gates of Hell? Could it be that they *will* unite and offer the Body and Blood of Jesus Christ in joint Sacrifice to save the world?

If Jews and Catholics were to unite in this Sacrifice, how easy it would be for the rest of Christendom to heed Gamaliel's counsel and respond to the prayer for unity addressed to the Mother of Jesus:

> "O Immaculate Virgin, who was preserved from Original Sin by a singular Grace, look down in pity upon our separated brethren who are still your children and call them back to the center of unity. Many have, even from afar, preserved a most tender devotion toward you, O Mother of Christ. Reward them for their devotion by obtaining the Grace of Conversion. Victorious over the powers of Hell from the very first moment of your existence, renew, now that the necessity is more urgent, your triumphal progress as in ages past. Glorify your Son, O Mother, by bringing

back to the one Fold His straying sheep, making them obedient to the guidance of the universal Shepherd, who is His Vicar on earth, to banish error from the earth, to put an end to disunity, and to restore peace to all Christian people. Amen."

℣. Our Lady of the Atonement, intercede for us.

℟. That the prayer of your Divine Son may be fulfilled; "That all may be one." Amen.

If God were to answer that Prayer for Unity after first uniting Jews and Catholics, what a multitude of vocations to the priesthood and to the Religious life would follow! The prayers of *The Marian Movement of Priests* would bring back those priests who have fallen into the hands of Satan and all would be set for that final show-down which God has planned since that day when He said: "I will establish a feud between thee and the Woman, between thy offspring and hers; she is to crush thy head, while thou dost lie in ambush for her heels." (Gen. 3:15).

All this could happen as a result of the prayers of those of us who wish to join the tidal wave of *menders* to plead for a swelling ocean of *menders* to pray: "Thy Kingdom come; Thy will be done on earth as it is in heaven." The depth of Faith that this would bring about would be the source of a wave of true vocations to the priesthood and a return to the traditional mode of Religious life where men and women would be recognizable in public as priests and nuns and brothers!

The theme of all my spiritual guidance has been based on the motto: *The Way of Perfection for All and Project Sainthood for Each.* All that you do, even to the tiniest detail, can be related to this motto. To the extent that you succeed, you will become a stalwart promoter of vocations and a defender of the Faith!

PRAYER TO THE BLESSED VIRGIN MARY FOR THE CONVERSION OF HER PEOPLE THE JEWS
(composed by the convert, Rabbi Paul Drach).

Dear Mother of the Messiah Jesus: you are our only Hope after Jesus. O glorious Queen of Heaven, O Virgin unstained by sin from the first instant of your existence, I have never called on you in vain. I beg you now to plead with your Divine Son Jesus to touch the hearts and minds of all Jewish People with grace from on high. Pray that in every place where Jews are living, the following words of your sublime Canticle may be heard and accepted:

"He has taken Israel by the hand, and has mercifully kept the Promise which He made to our forefathers - to Abraham and to his spiritual children in all nations until the end of time."

Any *quantity* of these cards may be obtained without charge from Reverend Arthur B. Klyber, C.s.s.R., Remnant of Israel, Box 400 Coarsegold, Cal. 93614

CHAPTER XIII
DANGER AND THE VOCATION OF MARRIAGE

Perhaps the most evil success of the anti-forces within the Church seeking demolition under the travesty of "renewal", has been the desecration of the Sacrament of Marriage. Here again, they have taken advantage of the wholesale example outside the Church and have been all too successful in detaching Marriage from the supernatural source of human dignity.

The Cana Conferences of former days, and hopefully some in our day, are desperately seeking to combat this evil and return to an appreciation of the sanctity of Marriage. It is obvious that marriages can best be protected from mediocrity by group sharing of ideas in an atmosphere which puts Marriage in its proper context; namely, a sacred and Sacrament-secured vocation sponsored by almighty God and intended by Him to be the central way of life designed to populate heaven. In other words, marriage happiness depends upon its identification with the religious setting in which God has intended it to flourish.

It is precisely because the tremendous industrial and scientific and, hence, materialistic advances of the twentieth century have tended to crowd Marriage out of that setting that marriage unhappiness has tended to mount out of all proportion during the same century. This has been intentionally aggravated in these years when renewal has been contaminated by so much that is false.

It is also precisely because these materialistic and pagan pressures are directed equally against all members of North American society, that those of us who admit that God has rights in the matter need to reinforce our appraisal of the whole situation by collaboration and mutual support. Cana experience has shown that this can best be done, not so much by spiritual guidance by the clergy alone, as by the mutual discussion of those sharing the vocation of Marriage in an atmosphere of Christian Charity promoted by the clergy.

And here, alas, it must be said that promotion of Cana discussion by the clergy must definitely exclude those priests who have made themselves ineligible by acts of disloyalty to the Magisterium. The number-one evidence of this disloyalty is, of course, expressed or implied dissent from the Encyclical, *Humanae Vitae*, of Pope Paul VI on artificial birth control.

But, given a loyal priest Moderator at a Cana Conference, he is advised to orient himself with the married couples attending with opening words something like this: "It is certainly obvious to you that I am not married. Furthermore, my parents, if they were living, would be happy to tell you that I was quite unsuccessful as a child. Thus, I am in no sense an expert on marriage or the family." Now, there are no *"rubrics"* attached to this last suggested sentence, but I am quite certain that it is supposed to be offered with a disarming smile that gives a hint that you are not expected to believe a word of it! It is, however, put that way as an introduction to the next sentence which very wisely assures the spouses present that they are the ones who must think and talk and pray togther about their marriage. So, for the remainder of this chapter, let us assume that I am addressing these married people.

All this is very sound advice, but it just happens that I am in a position to emphasize the smile that hints to you that your Parish Priest, celibacy and all,

Danger and the Vocation of Marriage 133

is an expert on Marriage and the family. There are two reasons for this. The first and most important one is that he is equipped by God with the Sacrament of Holy Order which is a lifelong drawing account of Sacramental Grace provided by Divine Providence to do what it takes to provide the counsel for which God has called him. His Sacramental Grace can help you to make the best use of your Grace of the Sacrament of Marriage.

The second reason for the dependability of your Parish Priest, you may be surprised to learn, *is* experience. You, I hope, have each had experience with only one spouse and that one of the sex opposite to your own and hence eternally somewhat obscure as to what makes it tick. A parish priest, on the other hand, even a young one, has had presented to him, in a way more intimate than spouses talk to each other, all the why and the wherefore of every item that needs to be known by spouses in good marriages, in bad marriages, and in wrecked marriages, in every stage of their evolution day after day all life long.

Now, it happens that I taught Canon Law for thirteen years at the Seminary of Christ the King at Westminster Abbey, British Columbia. Every fourth year we spent the entire course in the study of Catholic Marriage. I made it a point at the opening class of this course to assure my theologians that they would frequently meet with the taunt from those whom they are trying to counsel: "What possible right has a celibate Catholic priest got to tell people how to run their married life?" And I assured them, furthermore, that their acquaintance with me would permit them to state with confidence, that they knew one priest who insisted that he was better qualified as a marriage counsellor after six years in a seminary and twenty years of hearing confessions than he ever was from thirty years of delightfully happy married life.

It is to be hoped that each one of you will find that your Pastor and his assistants do deserve this confidence, but I agree with the suggestion that you can gain more skill in promoting marriage happiness by discussing its problems with each other in groups with a priest Moderator than you can by hearing them discussed by a Pastor or Moderator.

Now, in the Marriage Course in Canon Law and in counselling in the Rectory, a priest is perhaps more often dealing with problem marriages and marriage problems than he is with the happiest of marriages. And that, of course, is what I meant when I said that such experience gave me greater competence in solving problems than did the memory of happy marriage. That is *not* to say, however, that happy married life does not have many problems, but it *is* to say that the reason any marriage can be a happy marriage stems from the way its problems are met and solved.

In experimenting with chemicals we sometimes use mild solvents and at other times we use harsh precipitating materials which render compounds that are insoluble. In marriage, love is the universal solvent, selfishness is the universal elixir of insoluble trials.

Now, that word *love* is perhaps the most abused word in the English language and by it I do not mean the thousand-and-one misuses to which it is put. I mean that yearning compassion which Jesus Christ had for me which caused Him to offer Himself to torture because that was the remedy which was required for the cure of all the evil things that I am doing to sadden Him in the twentieth century.

Husbands and wives cannot equal that love in intensity, but they can and must try to practice it in kind, not just during the honeymoon, not until

Danger and the Vocation of Marriage 135

children begin to crowd life with distractions, not in the event of emergency and tragedy, but day-by-day and hour-by-hour all life long. The catalyst that makes that kind of love the universal solvent is the Grace of the Sacrament of Marriage and the container that keeps Grace potent is the soul refreshed by weekly Confession and Communion. There are no substitutes for these ingredients of happy marriage.

If you will discuss your marriage problems and questions in groups which constitute the laboratory of this kind of love, you can help each other immensely toward greater perfection in the vocation of Marriage. And it is just there that I believe that my thirty years of happy married life does give me a better perspective than any amount of time spent in dealing with problems that have not been successfully solved.

Each one should feel free to present for discussion any question pertaining to the vocation of Marriage which may be useful to others. There are, however, two wide-open fields of discussion which a Moderator should try to orient so as to avoid controversy and promote understanding.

The first discussion is posed by a question something like this: Father, the atmosphere in which we are living exerts a pressure which simply does not give time for quiet family life and the enjoyment of the companionship of each other. There are not nearly enough hours in the day for the things outside of family life that are expected of us and demanded of us if we expect to keep even in business, in society, in the doings of our Church. Every member of the family has a different program from morning till night. Almost all of the demands for our time are separating rather than uniting. What is the answer?

I doubt if there is a single spouse who is not bothered, at least a little by that question. It is simply a fact that we live in a world that is becoming increasingly pagan, increasingly materialistic, increasingly covetous, increasingly selfish, increasingly disobedient, increasingly indifferent to God. Every married couple in North America is experiencing this same pressure and, to very many of them, it is a source of tragic woe. To Catholic young people it is perhaps most perplexing because they, more than others, realize that Christian Marriage is a vocation that should take precedence over every other demand in this life of pressure.

And there, alone, is the answer! Every husband has a responsibility to provide for the temporal welfare of his family. But his exercise of this responsibility must always be regarded as *one* of the obligations of the vocation of Marriage rather than as a career which takes precedence when one or the other must suffer. Now this does *not* mean that a husband must neglect his job to save the fee of a baby-sitter, but it does mean that a husband may not allow the Catholic atmosphere of his home or his loving companionship with his family to languish in order to to become involved in business pursuits which would penalize either. Cana experience suggests that most men would do well, upon returning home, to pause a moment in the front yard (or in the elevator) and consciously remind themselves that here they are primarily husband and father.

The same, as regards the affairs of a non-domestic career, is even more binding upon a wife whose career as Catholic housewife is a profession higher in God's eyes than any other work she might undertake.

And for the rest, it can only be said that here there is a hierarchy of values which Catholics should learn to recognize. This is an age of specialization in which no one can possibly do all of the things that may seem to be inviting or even very useful. The tendency of materialism to seek after so-called "gracious living" must be kept in proper perspective by Catholic husbands and wives and the aim of Christian Marriage to bring souls to heaven must never be allowed to be superseded.

The second field of discussion which needs to be oriented to avoid controversy pertains to this decade of turmoil which has followed the Second Vatican Council. History shows that almost every General Council of the Church has stirred the Devil into a frenzy of hate in which he spares no pains to urge individual lay and clerical leaders of the Church to cast doubt on the moral and doctrinal teaching of the Church in any direction that may offer an opening. And the present decade is no exception. In other words, as Christ has warned us, the "Gates of Hell" will never cease to seek to prevail against the Sheepfold of Christ. *But they shall not prevail!*

This pressure always directs itself most vehemently against the most controversial issues of the century in which it finds itself. So now, contrary to the urgent commands of Pope John XXIII, Pope Paul VI, and Popes John Paul I and II, as well as all preceding popes, there are books, pamphlets, leagues, study clubs, and commentaries which do not even leave the Catholic press immune, seeking to cast doubt upon the scope of the Infallible Magisterium of the Church and, most particularly, upon the capacity to declare the Law of God with respect to conjugal love and conjugal chastity.

The year-after-year fountain of happiness in Marriage stems from its true status as a holy vocation powered by a Sacrament which guides the will on a supernatural level to take in its stride its sacrifices and its trials together with its joys. In that setting, sex becomes a power of so much wider scope than the mere physical act of generation that it would regard with utter contempt and disgust the state of mind which would separate it from its total function and make it into a sordid side-issue of selfishness and lust.

The bodies of the sacramentally married are holy places where God has a right to reign. There are, to be sure, chemicals and devices and practices which attempt to cheat God of that right. But how dearly do they pay for the momentary thrill which is all that is left for those who gauge life and love on such terms. The pressure of the world is all in that direction and very many unthinking souls are attracted by its glitter. Their behavior is a matter of God's judgment, not ours. But the sham of satisfaction which they achieve is a pitiful travesty of the glorious joy of those who heed the loving call of the Heart of Jesus and play God's game of life on God's terms.

There is one comment regarding conjugal love that is most often posed by the carnal minded to deny the right of celibate clergy to specify as to the decisions of individual conscience. It is most often expressed by the declaration that the maintenance of conjugal love *demands* frequent satisfaction of the sexual appetite and that to demand continence, even periodic, as the *only* choice available to those who must avoid childbirth, is to destroy the atmosphere of love in the family.

Now, the wholesale acceptance of that declaration comes straight out of Hell! I am one priest who can look every married person in the eye and tell them that in the depth of their heart they *know* that the mutual acceptance of sacrifice for a valid reason is *the* most potent source of mutual love and respect. And the Law of God is *the* most valid reason to accept personal sacrifice.

And right here, while we are still eye-to-eye, is the time to quench that often-quoted alibi that one is free from guilt if his *conscience* does not accept the law as from God. There is no such thing in the definition of "conscience" as the power to *determine* what is proper behavior. Correctly formed conscience, insofar as it is allowed by the will to function, is what might be called an inner voice, placed by God in the soul, to prompt the will as to what is right behavior and what is wrong behavior. It is not a power to change wrong to right howsoever Situational Ethics may declare the contrary.

Conscience is a power given by God to creatures possessing intelligence, to guide the will to observe the Law of God. One of the most important functions of conscience is to make one know his responsibility to be informed as to the Law of God. Deliberate ignorance of God's Law is really only one form of refusal to accept God's Law.

And refusal to accept God's Law involves another all-important source of happiness in Marriage, *The grace of God*. Grace, like conscience, has an aspect of supernatural power supplied by God to do what it takes to please God. And what pleases God will automatically please a spouse who is motivated by Grace.

And that brings up what is probably *the* greatest flaw in all marriages today: *absence or neglect of God's grace*. All the Sacraments are supplied with special Graces which enable them to function perfectly *if used*.

Sacramental Marriage, which is the only form of true Marriage available to Catholics, is equipped with special Sacramental Grace which amounts to a lifelong drawing account to enable each partner to do what it takes to meet *every* experience of every hour of married life. *All* the flaws and *all* the sorrows and *all* the trials of married life stem from failure of one or both spouses to *use* the Sacramental Grace of the Sacrament of Marriage. And, if this last paragraph is given careful thought by every Catholic spouse who reads it, this chapter on Marriage will meet much of the *danger* that besets us all!

CHAPTER XIV

ECCLESIAM SUAM
WARNS OF DANGER

In the decade since the close of the Second Vatican Council there has been much comment in the secular press and even in a number of Catholic publications which gives the impression that, at long last, the forward-looking members of the Catholic hierarchy are beginning to overcome the repressive tenacity of the old-line reactionaries which has made certain items of Catholic doctrine an insurmountable obstacle to all hope of Christian reunion. This propaganda has wrought much mischief which has not only defeated its own purpose, but has caused anxiety and misgivings in the hearts of many good Catholic people. Misinterpretation and misquotation of things that *have* been said and done have been twisted so as to give a semblance of authenticity to this notion and have done much harm to the welfare of souls.

This has brought about a spirit of criticism and disobedience and hostility which has penetrated even into the thinking of some of those who are God's ministers and there is danger of untold harm which could result from its perversity, even though many of the individuals infected by it may well be in good faith. Much of this harm, however, can be avoided if and when the rank and file of Catholic people, both lay and clerical, can become intrenched in a calm and docile conviction that the One, Holy, Catholic, and Apostolic Church is by no means on the verge of shattering changes made necessary by decay, but is still and always under the infinitely loving and all-sufficient protection of the truth-giving Spirit who *has* come and who *is* always guiding us into all truth.

There are, indeed, changes needed in the method

of expression of much of this truth in order to destroy its distortion and misinterpretation which has long been an obstacle to the unbeliever and to those who have grown up separated from the Church. The true and full presentation and not a watering-down of the doctrine is what our late Holy Father, Pope John XXIII, and our late Holy Father, Pope Paul VI, and our present pope, Pope John Paul II, have so earnestly urged all to seek. It is true that they have all urged dialogue which seeks to emphasize all that we have in common with other men. The reason for this is that very few, especially among Christians outside the Catholic Church realize how very much we do have in common with them.

But this very reason for the need of dialogue is very far from the assertion, made by some, that these popes have abandoned the caution commanded by Pope Pius XII in his instruction of January 12, 1950. He wrote warning the Bishops of the world to be on their guard, lest, as he put it, "Catholic tenets, be they dogmas or questions connected therewith, . . . are so whittled down and somehow made to conform to heterodox teaching as to jeopardize the purity of Catholic doctrine or obscure its clear and genuine meaning."

Pope John XXIII did, indeed, and with amazing and inspired determination, demand that we show the separated Christians how much of what they believe agrees with Catholic doctrine; and he insisted that we do it by dialogue initiated by our Church. But that is very far from attempting to make points of difference appear to agree, as the above quotation from Pope Pius XII warns.

The harm comes from those who maintain that Pope John and Pope Paul have repudiated this warning. Unfortunately it has been hinted that this notion is also held by some members of the Teach-

Ecclesiam Suam Warns of Danger

ing Authority of the Church and this has been repeated by those who are less informed and by the secular press whose motive is to arouse excitement at all costs, even though it may promote doubt and distress rather than security and peace.

Most readers would not be interested in a technical discussion of this apparent controversy, but you are and ought to be very much interested in a proper understanding of the utter stability of our Faith and our Church and the true attitude which we should have toward separated brethren derived from a docile, loving, confident trust in the teaching of our Popes, knowing that the truth into which they are guided by the Truth-Giving Spirit is not subject to diminution, error, or change.

And the reason that you should be involved in this aspect of the situation, aside from the inestimable importance for your own peace of mind, is that you, each one of you, is an important member of the Mystical Body of Christ and by your example of confidence and assurance you can do much to promote the welfare of the Church and offer a potent invitation to those outside who are truly seeking God.

It is almost impossible to over-estimate the importance of the example, for good or for harm, that each one of us exhibits, both to those within the Church and to those without. Remember the words of Saint Paul: "Speak ye the truth every man to his neighbor, since we are members one of another . . . and give no opportunity to the Devil." (Eph. 4:25-26). We definitely give opportunity to the Devil when we allow ourselves to be daunted by doubt as to the stability of the doctrine which has always been taught by our Church or when we share in insinuations that it can be "whittled down and somehow be made to conform to heterodox teaching", to use the words of Pope Pius XII.

It is to fortify all of us, then, in this regard that I wish to study with you just what has been said by our Holy Father of happy memory, Pope Paul VI, in his first and most timely Encyclical Letter called *"Ecclesiam Suam"* which opens with these words: "Since Jesus Christ founded *His Church* to be the loving Mother of all men and the dispenser of salvation, it is obvious why she has always been specially loved and cherished by those who have the glory of God and the salvation of men at heart."

Pope Paul carries this notion of the all-inclusiveness of the Church throughout the length and breadth of this Encyclical, stressing that it is all-inclusive because it was so designed by Christ and, if it does not at present include all men, it is not because of any defect in the divine plan and the divinely given composition of the Church, but because it is also a part of the divine plan that the *functioning* of the Church, even though divinely protected as to doctrine, will, nevertheless, reflect a composite of the free responses of all of the souls within and without, to the eternal invitation which it presents.

In other words, the trials which the Church has always faced and, as Christ has warned, it *will* always face, stem, not from defect of structure as established by Christ, but from imperfection in the human make-up of its cells and organs. That these imperfections exist today should be obvious to all. In fact, it should be obvious to us within the Fold that if every member of the Church perfectly fulfilled his office in accordance with the mind of Christ, the example of its inherent perfection would in truth and in fact draw all men to Christ.

It was, then, the purpose of Pope Paul, expressed in his Encyclical, *"Ecclesiam Suam,"* to invite and direct the Fathers of the Second Vatican Council to examine in a docile manner and in a spirit of poverty and charity as to just how the Church as designed and established by Christ can be made to effect perfectly its mission of salvation here and now. The structure provided by Christ is capable of perfect functioning. The gap between perfection and present functioning is the area in which the Council was called to bring its case before the world.

In other words, the Deposit of Faith, the form of sacrificial worship, the sacramental channels of grace, and the guardianship of the Holy Spirit are God-Given and need no change; their presentation to the men of the world has been commanded by Christ, and we have His word for it that they are adequate. It was, therefore, the duty and the chief purpose of the Fathers of the Council, who were the current recipients of the command of Christ, to examine the past and the present and determine what is necessary to make this presentation function as Christ has told us that it should.

It is, then, primarily the presentation of the Church and not its constitution that is at fault and in this Encyclical Pope Paul proposed that the correction of this fault be incorporated into the dialogue which the command of Christ makes it our duty to press always toward perfection.

And what does all this mean to each one of us individual members of the Mystical Body of Christ which is the Church? First of all, it should be intensely reassuring. It should quench in our hearts any tendency to be anxious about the apparent evils of our time and replace that tendency with a confidence replete with joy that we have been given by God the grace to share in this absolutely certain means of salvation provided for us by God. It should strengthen our resolve to cling confidently to that means so that its absolute certainty may embrace us, by God's help, all life long.

We have that "Pearl of Great Price" which Christ has offered us and let us enter into wholeheartedly and devotedly. If this devotion is truly wholehearted, it should make us anxious to do our utmost to aid the project of bringing it to all the rest of the world. In so doing we will promote our own individual Project Sainthood.

Over the altar in the chapel at Providence Hospital in Everett, Washington, where I have served as Chaplain, there is a baldachin which is encircled with the legend: "The Charity of Christ Urges Us." That legend should be deep in the heart of every member of the Catholic Church today. The decrees of the Council and its fruits for years to come, should fill us with a sense of urgency, not that the Council was called because there have been grave defects in former presentations of the invitation of Christ to all men, but rather that the Charity of Christ has built up a pressure that has invaded the heart of every true lover of Christ and urges him to use heroic effort to remove the shackles that may have kept His Heart from going out to all men.

With Christ's Charity urging us, then, let us see what we can find to fit our Project Sainthood to the message which we have received from our late Holy Father, Pope Paul VI. First, he wishes us to be utterly impervious to the anxiety which seems to be the objective of much that is reported in the secular press; to be utterly aloof from the spirit of rash innovation that incites disagreement and criticism and disobedience and distrust of the teaching Church; to be utterly compassionate and understanding of the difficulties of those outside the Church who have not yet been given the grace to see the truth which seems so obvious to us.

It is in this last respect that the renovation of the "face" of the Church will promote the dialogue of charity in which the decrees of the Council can be aided by the good will and the example of every Catholic. It can only be realized, however, by those who are free from anxiety and the spirit of disobedience. If, however, we are thus free and do possess these qualities, we can do much to promote the purpose which Pope Paul expressed as his will for the Council and for his Pontificate; namely, to show the importance of the Church for the salvation of mankind *and* her heartfelt desire that the Church and mankind should meet each other and should come to know and love each other.

This purpose, the Holy Father says, suggests three spheres of action. The first, which furnishes the motive for all the rest, is to try to match the great mystery of the Church which is its image in the mind of God, with the image of the living Church under God here and now. The actual present image of the Church is never as perfect, as lovely, as holy, or as brilliant as the formative divine idea would wish it to be. And this is the area where there is need for renewal and correction of defects as if looking in a mirror.

And this suggests the second sphere of action: to find a way to achieve wisely such a sweeping renovation within the household of the faith. This second sphere of action involves the momentous changes in the liturgy which have had for their objective the incorporation of the people of God more closely into the communion of worship. And then the third sphere, to determine the relationships which the Church should establish with the world in which it works.

One rather sad circumstance concerns that great part of the world which surrounds us in North America. It is the part that has lost or is fast losing the recognition of the fact that it owes its greatest gifts to Christianity and has detached itself from the Christian foundations of its culture. This, alas, is the status of almost all of North America. It is more indifferent than hostile and is only faintly receptive of friendly dialogue. Nevertheless, it is this dialogue that must be solved within the decrees of the Council; its urgency is a burden, a stimulus, a vocation in which every one of us who is loyal to the love of Christ must have a part, particularly by prayer and by example.

We can equip ourselves for this by remembering the admonition of the Divine Founder of the Church to be ever watchful of ourselves and docile to the will of God that we may develop the consciousness sought by Saint Paul for the Philippians when he said to them: "May your love grow richer and richer yet, in the fullness of its knowledge and the depth of its perception." (Phil. 1:9).

Thus equipped, we, each one, can aid the post-conciliar organization and the Pope in inviting all men to make a loving, profound, and conscious act of faith in Jesus Christ our Lord which our Holy Father, Pope John Paul II in his encyclical *The Redeemer of Man*, says is especially appropriate at this moment, which he calls a unique moment in the life of the Church. It is unique in the life of the Church because the Church is bound up in mankind and mankind is undergoing transformations, upheavals and developments which, to use the words of *Ecclesiam Suam*, "profoundly change not only exterior modes of life, but its way of thinking." And this, Pope Paul VI says, must involve the whole Church and he warns: "Men committed to the Church are greatly influenced by the climate of the world, so much so that a danger bordering almost on dizzy confusion and bewilderment can shake the Church's very foundations and lead men to embrace most bizarre ways

Ecclesiam Suam Warns of Danger

of thinking, as though the Church should disavow herself and take up the very latest and untried ways of life."

If this be true; and we only need to glance at the folly of Modernism, Rationalism, Materialism, and the so-called Situational Ethics, to be convinced of it; can you not see why the Holy Father tells us that the remedy is for the Church to deepen her awareness of what she really is according to the mind of Christ? The Holy Spirit will, indeed, still function if we will but listen. And docility to His guidance will enable us to make divine truth an argument for union and not a reason to divide men into sterile discussions and regrettable divisions. He will enable us, instead, to help men to a renewed discovery of the vital bond of union with Christ in His Church.

There is untold treasure and richness of grace in this great mystery which is ours as a result of mature and living faith. Pope Paul reminds us of the exultant joy with which we should regard the treasure of the Sacrament of Baptism which binds us and builds us in as units of the Edifice erected by Christ on the Rock, Peter, whom Christ had miraculously transformed from weakness to be the pillar and ground of truth.

The Church is, and always will be, subject to human frailty. Nevertheless, we should know by this time that this is as God intended it to be. How else can we interpret these ominous words of Christ: ". . . you shall be hated by all the nations for My Name's sake. And then many shall fall away; and they will betray one another, and hate one another. And many false prophets will arise and mislead many. And on account of the increasing lawlessness, the love of the majority will be chilled. But he who perseveres to the end, he it is who shall be saved.

And this gladdening news of the Kingdom shall be proclaimed throughout the whole world, as an evidence to all nations." (Matt. 24:9-14).

I beg you not to regard these words, or the admonitions of Pope Paul, as abstract platitudes! We, dear people, are living in a tremendous age as regards mankind and the Church. Each one of us is deeply concerned and has a part to play and a tremendous treasure at stake. Our first reaction should be one of joy and realization that the great doings of this age and of the Council are evidence that the Holy Spirit of God has the matter very much in hand!

Our second reaction should be one of gratitude to God for the splendid adequacy of the Popes He has given us during the past century. There was a time when God allowed the papacy to suffer a devastating interior decay with exterior jeopardy to the very life of the Church for several centuries. Its survival was a miracle of God's power. Now, the times are different and God again shows His power by choosing men each exactly suited to the needs of his particular pontificate. And this great Encyclical, *His Church*, shows Pope Paul VI to be no exception.

Let us, then, each of us, couple our Project Sainthood to Pope Paul's wishes for us when he tells that Christian life will always require faithfulness, effort, mortification, and sacrifice. . . . It will require opposition to the spirit of the world, discipline, opposition to the laxity of modern behavior, alertness to the contradictions of modern thought. The Christian today is not soft and cowardly; he is strong and faithful. Let us each do our part by renewing and continuing our prayers for the success of the acts of the Council and by the example of our lives, which Pope Paul tells us, is even more potent than preaching!

CHAPTER XV

CHARITY SHIELDS FROM DANGER

In the previous chapter we have tried to inspire in the heart of each and every Catholic, clerical and lay, the will to become, by prayer and example and action, a stalwart defender of the Faith and an apostle of good will to all men. Now, to promote individual enthusiasm for this project, it is my hope to fortify every reader with a deep appreciation of the *Charity of Christ* for each individual soul, since that is the all-inclusive motive for all religion.

We have discussed the army of traitors within the Church who have distorted doctrine, down-graded devotion and driven distrust and doubt into the hearts of all too many priests and people. All this has built up the *danger* faced by all of us. In order to make us effective workers against this *danger* we must learn to use the shield of Christ's Charity which meets and conquers every danger!

Saint Paul's immortal Thirteenth Chapter of First Corinthians clinches the necessity of our Charity toward God and man. But the foundation and source of all Charity is the infinite love demonstrated by Jesus Christ and its application to each individual soul as if to him alone.

The Way of the Cross shouts this infinite love and should clinch in each of us a response that is proof against all doubt. My prayer at the First Station sets the pattern for me "Lord Jesus Christ, I stand with You before Pontius Pilate and beg you to give me a glimpse of the infinite gratitude we owe to You for creating this universe and giving us being in this world. And when we had botched our part, You came and submitted to our torture for no other reason than Your infinite love for me and for all men. Give me the Grace to respond to that love with the limit of human capacity to love You and to *trust* You!"

And again, at the Second Station I pray: "Lord Jesus Christ, Who accepted the Cross of Crucifixion because of Your love for me and because of my infinite need, I beg You to give me the Grace to accept with gratitude *whatever* You choose for me and to know that whatever happens *is* what You choose for me. And when there are trials, give me the Grace to accept *them* with gratitude so as to prove my love and to build my love for You."

Christ could have made possible our salvation without ever leaving the splendor of His heavenly home. But, having made the unbelievable decision to take upon Himself our human nature, He could have redeemed us by the slightest act of reparation. And even when it was decreed by the eternal God-head that a bloody sacrifice of reparation should be made, He could have satisfied such a decree by shedding one drop of His most precious Blood as ample satisfaction for all the sins of the world. But why, then, did He choose the ignominy and torture of the Cross? It was to show us the infinite malice of sin, the infinite love of Christ for each one of us and the infinite invitation for us to love Him.

As Christ is nailed to the Cross, it is impossible for us to conceive the depth of the riches of the love that prompted this unheard-of pinnacle of generosity without true contrition for our sins for which He suffered and a love that breeds true hatred for the slightest sin and fills our hearts with true Charity, loving Christ for Christ's sake with all our heart and soul and mind and strength.

I kneel before the Tabernacle as a Fifteenth Station and say: "Lord Jesus Christ, risen from the dead and imprisoned here in the Tabernacle because of Your love for me, I beg you to give me the Grace to return your love with the limit of my capacity to adore You, to worship You, to be at-one with You in all that I do and think and say."

And that reminds me of a facet of prayer which Jesus has put into my heart in recent days which has completely changed the nature of all of my prayer and helped to drive out distractions. All of my prayer used to be *me* speaking to the Father or to Jesus or Mary full of Grace or to a saint. It was I praying into the air and trying to mean it. Then, all at once, it came to me that vocal prayer means nothing unless it is heard by the one who is addressed. Now my prayer is all to a listening Father within my soul, to a listening Christ in the Tabernacle, to a listening Virgin Mary making present the love of Jesus for all who pray to her or to the saints. The change of stance is tiny but the difference is immense! And with practice, it can make almost every thought a prayer.

The words of Christ reported in the little paperback, *He & I*, published by Editiones Paulines, of Sherbrooke, Quebec, make this listening presence of Christ a constant joy. For example, on January 16, 1947, He said to the Mystic: "I am like Sampson; I lose My power as judge when someone tells Me of his faithful love. Not because the love is so great either, but because it is the greatest he has to offer Me. It touches Me to the quick and I am ready to bend to his will and make it My own."

And again, on December 26, 1946: "Be one with Me and believe that this pleases Me . . . And nothing on earth can give you an idea of what this oneness is that I ask of you. It is God's oneness; that means oneness of a love above every other love. I alone can help you find it. So think of this and ask Me for it. Above all, don't be afraid of loving Me. Don't you know that the more you love, the happier you are? Because this is your end, the end for which you are created. Don't you feel that you are made to love Me?"

"Repeat to yourself often, 'I believe in Your love for me, in Your boundless love. I know that You have loved me with an everlasting love.'" And I know, from daily experience, that the reader will profit by following that request of our Lord. And He clinches it by saying: "I need each one of you as though you were the only person in the world, as though the cosmos had been created for you alone, and My love is greater than the cosmos. So let this thought be a strength to you and your smiling calm." (Mar. 6, 1947).

Christ, in His parables suggested the idea of comparing our Faith to a plant which, when fully matured and deep of root, will bear for each one of us our eternal harvest of Charity. There are, however, some practical obstacles standing in the way of this happy fruition of Faith. I mention this, not to cloud our enjoyment in contemplating the love of God, but to emphasize its preciousness and to help us to avoid even the slightest loss of the riches which we are striving for all life long in what Saint Benedict calls this "School of the Lord's Service."

This precious harvest of Charity which we are here to win is held by us in earthen vessels. We regard with amazement those who are indifferent or, still more, those who seem to throw away the treasure they have once held. We should remember that these catastrophes to souls begin by little and little. Any small infidelity in our own affection could easily be the start of the ruin of our own lives. Saint Bonaventure says: "Our affection is the intention of our will which gives the quality of all our work." And Father McGarrigle comments: "The will of God is the gold in the coin of our action. The same form of coin with the metal of any other will in it is worthless." (*My Father's Will*, p. 90). And so our acts may look most holy, even to ourselves, but they are worse than worthless unless their motive is free from the base-metal of self-will. "What*ever* you do, perform from the heart as for the Lord, and not for men; knowing that from the Lord you shall receive the reward of the inheritance." (Col. 3:23-24).

The love of God is the only sufficient motive for every vocation in life. You may never have asked yourself the specific question: "Why am I here?" But the answer is perhaps *the* most important item in the life of each one of us. The answer hinges on three ideas which I want to try to make the theme of each of our lives as we study the notion that *Charity Shields from Danger*.

The first idea is this: The only motive worth its salt for every thought and word and act of every Christian soul should stem from the fact that you believe with all your heart that Jesus Christ is God; you love Him for the length that He has gone to to save your soul and you want to show that love in everything you do.

The second idea springs from the first and is this: The perfect response of the love which is born of the motive of faith in the Godhood of Jesus Christ is the donation of one's self, body and soul, to the service of Christ, whatever may be one's vocation in the world. And, of course, that means, for those who are free to do so, the realization that there is nothing in this world (or forever) so precious for the men and women in it as the priesthood or the life of a Religious. But whatever may be your vocation, the same idea has equal force and incentive.

The third idea again, springs from the other two. It is this: Renunciation of your own will and conformity to the will of God is the only sure means of persevering in *any* vocation, even though it does spring from a love of God caused by a pure faith in the divinity of Christ.

These ideas should seem very simple to every Catholic. But let us turn them over and take them apart and try to see just how our thoughts and words and acts conform to these ideas. Having done that, we may be able to put together a course of action which will help us to lead better lives on surer, safer ground.

Every true Catholic believes without a doubt that Christ is God. But how intense and deep and realistic is that faith? There was a time fairly long ago when every *Christian* believed the same thing. But that time is now over.

The growing materialism of our day; the growing sentiment that the tremendous strides of scientific research have demolished the certainty of the supernatural; the skepticism of the superficial scientists and so-called philosophers in our colleges, have undermined the faith of all too many. Now, with many non-Catholics "Christian" is becoming only a name. And with some, those who are most thoughtful, it is openly admitted that the manner of their lives and the human tenets to which they wish to cling, are utterly inconsistent with the honest belief that Christ is God.

Realizing this, they are beginning to allow their behavior to conform to the hollow insincerity of their waning faith, and have allowed themselves to accept the notion coined by the really evil haters of Christ who have spread the name of Christ as "The Myth".

These haters of Christ are really haters of the moral law of Christian behavior. They have deliberately set out to shatter the only valid sanction for morality, that of divine authority. The obvious first step has been to destroy the acceptance of the Bible as an

Charity Shields From Danger

historical document. To do this they have used the findings of experimental psychology to claim that the Bible, especially the New Testament, is a scientifically interesting myth, put together as a result of the wishful thinking of a persecuted group of fanatics two or three hundred years after the defeat, death and burial of the Man, Jesus of Nazareth. This theory has been demolished by other scientists who have verified the age of the ancient documents from which the New Testament has been assembled. It is, however, no less preposterous than the theory of evolution which the Atheists must hold against the billion-fold proofs of the necessity of creation.

It seems incredible that such a theory could have gained acceptance, even among people willing and ready to repudiate the moral law. It probably would have been impossible, except for the fact that scientific research has lent itself to the support of crass materialism with its flat denial of the supernatural. And so, practically all of the attacks on the Bible have been based on the *a priori* assumption that no report of a supernatural event has any historical validity. With every contrary proof dismissed, they have taken what little is left of the New Testament and each one has felt free to try his hand at concocting a plausible explanation of the drab events of the life of Jesus of Nazareth which have led to the amazing myth, claiming that He was God, incarnate Creator of the universe!

To the reader it may seem doubly incredible that such nonsense could gain wide acceptance. But that is because, thank God, Holy Mother Church has done all in her power, and has been helped by the Holy Spirit, to shelter you from the blast of these attacks. Many Catholics, especially young people, have not been so fortunate. The poison of this attack is so deceitful; the lust of the flesh is so alluring; the wiles of Satan are so treacherous, that constant vigilance is needed to keep us from contamination. The worst of it is that contamination from this poison can be almost imperceptible in its beginning.

You would understand this better if you were aware of what is going on in our secular universities, East and West. On the other hand, you may have had this experience and know how the "Myth" theory is insinuated by far too many of the professors, so that it gradually gains acceptance, not only by the weight of its constant repetition, but also by the condescending attitude toward Catholic Students, as if they were the stupid dupes of clever priests who keep them blinded from the facts of the world of science.

I knew a young man who was a graduate of the College of Forestry in one of our western State Universities. His mother was a devout Catholic and she told me, with tears, how faithful he had been as a boy and up to the time of entering the University. He carried a paper delivery route during his grammar school days and often he would get up half an hour early so he could complete his route in time to attend the weekday Mass at the Catholic Church near his home.

When I knew him he was a State Forester, living a short half-mile from our summer home where daily Mass was open to to the public. The Chaplain and I had both urged him to come to Mass, but he always refused. At length his mother died in a distant city and the Chaplain called upon the young man and offered to say a Requiem Mass for his mother at the time of her funeral if he would attend. He came and sat without genuflecting, bolt upright at the back of the chapel and left immediately after the Mass and never returned.

You may think there must have been some other

Charity Shields From Danger

reason, but no. That young man had been robbed of his faith by the sneering persecution of his professors in biology, chemistry and geology at the University. I have seen a very similar tragedy enacted at one of the other State Universities in the West, where the head of the Philosophy Department was an apostate priest.

No Catholic suddenly decides that he cannot believe that Christ is God. But we are intimately surrounded by people who believe themselves to be reasonably good people; who even think that they believe in the divinity of Christ; and yet their words and actions are utterly inconsistent with that belief. It is too easy to copy them without ever stopping to think that our words and actions imply a denial of our very faith in Christ; not to mention the adoring love that such a faith should engender.

The reader may wonder why I should be burdening you with the tragic lives of people who are so very far away. It is because none of us can be altogether free from this danger. Even when most of our contacts are with holy people, there is a *danger* of humanizing our love and our motive for faith instead of divinizing it as it should be. The love of God in our hearts is always in danger of contamination from the people in the world whose love is so often selfish. And you, dear reader, may not realize how God allows one to become blinded when he is slow to cooperate with Grace. I know, because for almost half of my life I have been one of them.

I was more than forty years of age before God gave me the Grace to see that it is nonsense to think of Christ as God Who has founded a Church which has failed, even though you attribute the failure to human misbehavior. Seeing that, however, there is only *one* choice left; give up all religion or become a Catholic. Thank God, He let me choose rightly.

Far too many, however, do not even see that there is only one choice. They drift into irreligion because it is the course of least resistance. So, too, they practice at least a part of the moral law because they copy without thinking, the tradition of the past, when almost everyone tried to behave for the love of God or for the fear of Hell. They copy some of Christian goodness because they are, at least to some extent still surrounded by us, just as *we* are in danger of copying some of their badness because we are surrounded by them.

How can we avoid contamination by this poison? Well, the first step is to admit that it is present. The greatest danger of all is to consider ourselves immune. You are not altogether safe. I am not altogether safe. None of us ever will be altogether safe. By ourselves, we are very badly in need of help. And why is this? For the very reason that this is an evil which can only be vanquished by supernatural means.

Our only hope is to cultivate and cling to that love of Christ which is the first idea we have set out to make a part of the very fiber of our being, together with a sense of the preciousness of Life With God and the efficacy of conforming to the will of God.

We, in a Monastery, all think that we do love Christ most faithfully. Indeed, we do love Him or we would certainly not be here! But let us, together with every reader of these lines, ask ourselves this question: Have I ever done anything that I would not have done if I could have seen Christ in His human form, standing in front of me with out-stretched arms? Have I ever failed to do what I know my Faith requires of me, and what I would have done, if I could have seen Christ looking down at me from the Cross? Not one of us can claim a perfect score in this regard! And yet we know that He is really present to

Charity Shields From Danger

us *always*. As long as we are in a state of Grace, He is, with the Father and the Holy Spirit, dwelling within our very souls and making our body His temple. In fact, He is present to us as we are to ourselves. Do we always treat our bodies, and those of our neighbors, as we would treat Christ in the tabernacle? And, speaking of the tabernacle; how do we use the great privilege which we enjoy, of visiting with Christ in His divine substance which we clearly see with the eye of Faith? Do we make this a means of showing our love for Him?

Now, I am not urging the reader to invent any new devotions or to try to show up your neighbor by out-doing him in acts and words of love. But I do urge you to ask yourself if your acts and words concerning your neighbor, especially the one whom you least admire, are those which you would choose to show your love for Christ in him. I am not hinting either, that your love of Christ should show itself in something that you can feel or see. Sensible consolation may sometimes be the fruit of love, but it is of little importance and may even be a dangerous incentive to self-love. It is not a fertile source of love. True love, as I have stated, stems from the intellect and will. It comes from a fervent and ever-repeated act of Faith that Christ is God and is worthy of *all* our love.

Getting down on one's knees is not absolutely necessary to prayer. It may be only an imitation of prayer. But what I want with all my heart that each reader should get out of this chapter and this book, is that the sure road to love is to prostrate the soul in constant adoration before Christ our King. Getting on one's knees may help the soul to adore, but we do not need to wait for the times we can kneel, in order to pray.

Cultivate the habit of praying always. Never tire

of telling Christ that you love Him! Ask Him for Grace to be remembering your love for Him whether you work or study or recreate or eat or when you are lying down to sleep. Never miss a chance to tell Him so, especially when He is before you on the altar. Learn to be increasingly reverent toward the Sacramental Presence of God. Get the habit of making little ejaculations of love. Jesus mercy! All for Thee, my Jesus! Thy will be done! I love you, Jesus!

Ask Mary to help you to love Him more. Never get the idea that this kind of prayer is emotional. It is all right to keep it to yourself, but never underrate the power of this constant prayer of love. If you get this habit here and now, it will bear fruit all your life long, because there will never be a time when you will not need it. May God bless each one of you with the Grace to love Him more. And may His Charity shield you from the *danger* that surrounds all of us and *save your faith and mine!*

CHAPTER XVI

A MESSAGE FOR EVERYONE
ADDRESSED TO DIVORCED CATHOLIC WOMEN

What could be a greater calamity, tragedy, disaster? What could happen to you that would be greater agony, frustration, desolation—especially to a *Catholic* wife who seems to be cut off *by* her Faith from everyone who can give her help or hope or harmony of goal? Every source of joy is shattered!

All this seems to be gravely true. But it is because you have been gravely cheated, perhaps all life long, of true and supernatural possession of your Catholic Faith. It is almost certain that every Catholic Marriage that fails is the result of a pitiful lack of knowledge of the true meaning and purpose of God's relationship to us provided by His Church. And because that pitiful cheating of true Faith is so wide-spread, it seems to you that what I am telling you is nonsense.

It might take months or years of study and instruction to give you certain knowledge that what I say is absolute truth. *But,* if you are willing to make use of the months and years that I have spent to make me *know* what I am telling you, I can put you on a course in ten minutes that will change the whole aspect of the disaster that you seem to be facing. All it takes is a little act of your will to accept the following truth: However deserted and betrayed and misunderstood you may feel at this moment, God loves you with a love that is so great that you cannot possibly understand it. It is absolutely true that His love for you alone is as if He had created this universe and founded His Church and suffered His Crucifixion so that you alone could be united in love with Him forever in heaven. And that is true even if you are now, and know that you are now in a state of sin that has, in effect, crucified Jesus Christ and closed your soul to His abiding presence.

Admittedly, that seems impossible but it is true and God has made it possible for us to know that it is true. His Church and His Vicar on earth, the Holy Father, are provided by God to make us able to know that it is true. Furthermore, He has given each one of us a conscience which gives us the capacity to know what is God's choice for our response to His love for us. Conscience is *not* a capacity to *decide* what is right behavior in response to God's love. It is, as I have said, a precious gift from God to make us able to know God's choice. We may *ignore* the voice of conscience and even deny it to ourselves and to others. But conscience is still there and God will not compel us to heed this voice.

All sin is choosing self instead of God. It is unbelievable in the abstract, but fallen man, with Satan's help, is doing many unbelievable things in these days.

Above all, I want you to remember this: The Catholic Faith, well understood, is *the* greatest treasure one can own in this world. All else is incidental. Without it, nothing else counts. With it, nothing else matters. It is the means chosen by God to give you and me the eternal happiness for which God created the universe. Any other religion is a manmade makeshift and not God's choice. If it does lead to heaven, it is only because God in His mercy allows the Catholic Church to save non-members who are not guilty of rejecting it knowingly. That is why the imperfect training of Catholics which leads to their failure in the high vocation of Marriage is a grave injury to their welfare.

So, you may ask *what to do about it?*

What I am going to place *first* would disappoint you by itself. But I ask you to believe me that with-

A Message to Everyone

out this *first* of mine, you are not prepared to cope with the things that are first in your mind at this moment. So, listen to my *first* and know that I am aware of your thoughts as expressed in a paragraph of a letter written by the National Director of the Judean Society for Divorced Catholic Women, which reads in part as follows:

> "The Catholic divorcee is severely tempted. To mention just a few of the burdens she faces at that time: Shame; guilt; humiliation; lack of religious education to make an adult moral decision; economic depression; emotional depression; taking full responsibility for a one-parent family; explaining to the children why Daddy doesn't come home any more. Then, to add to all this; clergy, religious and some of our bishops, tempt her with sexual temptations in the mixed groups of Divorced Catholics that they so widely advertise and encourage. How can she help but think that the Church has changed her laws, and now divorce is OK and she can seek the companionship of the opposite sex, and with the approval of the Church?
>
> With the subtle teaching of Satan's "Situation Ethics", found in these groups, I no longer wonder, but know, why so many Divorced Catholics leave the Church, (Christ in the Eucharist) to seek another union which will at least offer them the security of a man, and money. What a terrible mess their innocent ignorance gets them into. We *must* mend the mess of divorce!"

And before we go further, if you are not already acquainted with what Saint Jude has to offer to Divorced Catholic Women in *The Judean Society Inc.*, I suggest that you immediately write for information to: Mrs. Frances A Miller, National Director, The Judean Society, Inc., 1075 Space Park Way #336, Mountain View, California 94043.

But before you hear from Mrs. Miller, I want to try to clinch you to a real help that the Catholic

Faith can give you even while you are learning it.

So, here is my *First:* Even if you feel certain that you are not guilty of any unforgiven sin: *Go to Confession* with a brand new attitude of seeking the Sacramental Grace of the Sacrament of Reconciliation to fortify you with that certain knowledge that God Himself is *present* in your soul and ready to help you every time you turn to Him.

Try to know for certain that as long as you remain in spiritual Partnership with God, He will manage everything *perfectly*. All that happens is under His control and He who loves you more than you can possibly love Him, will give you the Graces to meet everything that happens, in Partnership with Him.

This is *most important.* Constant awareness of the presence and availability of God in your soul is necessary to enable you to enter with success the new way of life which you are facing. You are indeed placed in a new role in society and your present status resembles in some respects the novices entering religious life who are addressed by Cardinal Basil Hume in his excellent new book entitled: *Searching for God.* He says to them and to you:

> "The difficulties on your path to God should be put before you. Now one of the greatest of these difficulties is the apparent absence of God. I shall be surprised if within the next twelve months you do not at some time or other experience this. It is one of the greatest trials we undergo. It is, of course, at these moments that we seek an escape—into work, into social life: Any number of escape routes are available. Let me remind you that when you feel God's absence, Christ our Lord, our Model and our Hope, experienced just this. There is a rhythm of light and darkness. Happily the memory of light enables us to support the darkness, to look forward to the reemergence of light. For there *is* light, and plenty of it. It comes by the initiative of God Himself. Our task is to

be faithful, to persevere, to respond. In proportion as we give, in proportion as we commit ourselves, in proportion as we pray and are humble, in proportion as we draw closer to God, He will bless us and guide us."

The author then goes on to quote the opening words of the Rule of Saint Benedict:

"Listen, my brothers, I have something to tell you. I have a way of life to teach you. Listen to me with an open heart and mind. If you follow my instructions obediently and faithfully, you will find Him who is the Source of all your desires, the very one you have bypassed by going your selfish way."

Your first thoughts may be: Father doesn't understand we can't be expected to behave like monks and nuns! No, I am not asking you to behave like nuns! I am telling you what I know to be a *state of mind* that will bring you success in a role very different from that of a nun, but precisely the same in its need for Partnership with God.

And I emphasize this so you will not be still further dismayed by the next thing I advise you to do. And that is to know that the surest way to make your Catholic Faith your true possession, is to go to Mass and receive Communion as often as you possibly can! The way to approach this suggestion is to try to realize that it is not a burden or a sacrifice I am suggesting, but a priceless privilege which God in His love has provided for you. It is the way provided by God to clinch your awareness of that constant Partnership with God which is essential for peace and serenity in your new way of life.

If you have accepted the notion that frequent Confession and week-day Mass and Communion as often as possible, is the normal way to live in God's world, you will soon find in it a source of joy and strength that will change your whole attitude from frustration and distress to courage and confidence.

Next, in order to help you to make it *real* in your soul, I recommend *Prayer*. If you thoroughly believe in the reality of God's presence in your soul, you will find it easy to cultivate a companionship which will amount to constant prayer which can be carried on regardless of whatever else you may be doing or however absorbing your work or play or conversation may be. God will manage it all to your delight and to the joy of those with whom you associate.

There are, of course, almost millions of formal prayers that have been devised. The one which stands out above all others and the one which has the greatest weight with God, is the one devised by God-The-Son: Our Father who art in heaven . . . Another one that practically comes from heaven is the Hail, Mary. That makes the daily praying of the *Rosary*, as recommended by Our Lady of Fatima, the surest way of pleasing God and of working for the welfare of the world.

If you have never tried to pray the Rosary or have abandoned it because of distractions or for any other reason, please forget the past and *decide* that from now on you will pray the Rosary every day because you have discovered a new way to make it precious. That way is: Say the words really addressed to the members of the Holy Trinity present in your soul and to Mary who, with them, hears and treasures every word. *And* believe Christ's promise that every word you pray has *eternal value* which you will receive with amazement when you enter heaven! I rejoice to pray fifteen decades of the Rosary every day and, next to Mass and Communion, it is my greatest treasure.

Of the many other prayers and litanies that all help to keep one close to God, I find the following *Morning Prayer* most helpful to put the day in God's hands:

A Message to Everyone

MORNING PRAYER

O my God * my only good, and the Author of my being *
I give Thee my heart.

Praise, honor and glory be to the holy & undivided Trinity * now and forever more.

Come, O Holy Spirit, replenish my heart *
and enkindle in me the fire of Thy divine love.

O Eternal God, Father, Son and Holy Spirit * the beginning and end of all things, in whom we live and move and have our being.

I firmly believe that Thou art here present.

Grant that I may adore Thee with the most profound humility.

I praise Thee and give Thee thanks from the bottom of my heart * for having created and redeemed me.

For having hitherto preserved me *
and brought me safe to the beginning of this day.

I consecrate myself entirely to Thy most Sacred Heart, *
and will love Thee henceforth above all things.

Bestow on me, O sweet Savior, the abundance of Thy heavenly grace.

Behold, O Lord, I offer Thee my whole being, *
in particular my thoughts, words and actions.

Bless my work and all my undertakings * that they may tend to the greater honor of Thy sovereign majesty.

Preserve my heart from every sin *
and keep me from all dangers and accidents.

Guide me safely, O Lord, through the perils of this life, *
and grant me the grace of perseverance and a happy death.

Holy Mother of God, my advocate and patroness, *
pray for thy poor servant.

O sweet Virgin Mary, show thyself a Mother to me, *
keep and defend me as thy own.

Saint Joseph, my glorious patron, pray for me.

Dear Guardian Angel, whom God has appointed to watch over me, intercede for me this day * that I may not stray from the path of virtue.

O Jesus, have mercy on the souls in Purgatory.

Enlighten my mind, purify my heart, and guide my steps ° that I may pass all my life in Thy divine service. Amen.

If you will try all this out with real conviction that it is worth a million times what it costs, God will let you learn that your Catholic Faith will become very different from the picture of it that is presented to the world today and as it has been in your own mind in the past. You will revel in its treasure while you learn its true nature.

And now for one or two of the obstacles:

First: Remember that by the infinite wisdom of God, the Sacrament of Marriage is for life. If our fallen nature makes separation necessary, it can only be saved from disaster for each spouse by the certain knowledge that the supernatural bond is far more real than any item of practical living. Civil divorce has no effect on that bond but it does furnish certain natural protection.

If you have entered a valid Sacramental Marriage, you are a married woman as long as your spouse is alive. Therefore, separation means celibacy. If you will make that a definite part of your knowledge in your Partnership with God, He will give you the grace to diminish or banish temptation. You will automatically omit occasions of temptation such as mixed social events for divorced Catholics. I cannot imagine anything more deliberately dangerous.

Beyond that, my only advice is to try to cultivate a way of life that will occupy more than all of your time and keep you loaded with activity. Whatever your talents may be, or your capacity to help others—stretch them to the limit. In this regard, help for the Judean Society for Divorced Catholic Women, will certainly be amply rewarded by God. And remember, His reward is *eternal*!

And finally, do everything you do, definitely in the Presence of God and in Partnership with Him. And know too, that I will pray for you every day.

Warning: In these days, Satan, in a frenzy of hate, has daunted the souls of many priests causing them to give false advice regarding the laws of Marriage in defiance of the Pope and his Teaching Authority. Do not allow yourself to be misled by them *and know that God's love will guide you!*

A NOTE REGARDING NULLITY IN CATHOLIC MARRRIAGE

There is no such thing as divorce from valid, holy, Sacramental and consummated marriage. If a marriage breaks down and separation seems inevitable the Diocesan Matrimonial Tribunal of the Church should first be consulted for help. If nullity is found and decreed, then a civil divorce may be needed to clarify the civil status of the persons concerned. But a civil divorce has no effect whatsoever on the married state of the spouses.

In these days, the pitiful uninstructed state of all too many Catholic young people, sometimes brings it about that the marriage ceremony is performed without conferring the Sacrament and no marriage exists. The intended marriage is null and void and so it may be said that "a state of nullity exists" and though the couple may have been living together for a long time they are unmarried.

In such cases, a "Decree of Nullity" may be issued by the Diocesan Matrimonial Tribunal where the couple has lived. This Marriage Court examines the evidence and if the evidence *proves* that no marriage exists, a Decree of Nullity is issued. Then, and only then, is either one of the spouses free to marry. It is at this stage that a civil divorce is usually necessary.

Although God is the Author of Marriage, the Sacrament of Marriage is administered by the bride and groom, each to the other. It then becomes a three-way Bond between a man, his wife and God, binding for life and equipped by God with Sacramental Grace adequate to meet any and every problem that may arise *if* it is used with Faith. The Church is concerned with the proper administration of the Sacrament and with the future life and happiness of the husband and wife. This could be called a pastoral concern. Her specific function at the marriage ceremony is to *witness* and *assist* in conferring the Sacrament validly.

During the centuries which followed the machinations of King Henry VIII of England, the civil authority gradually intruded itself into the sacred alliance and assumed authority in the contract asserting this authority as giving the State power to cancel the contract. This usurpation of authority in regard to the marriage contract has gradually become established throughout the western world. It should be very clearly understood, however, that the exercise of this authority by the State to cancel the civil contract of marriage has absolutely no effect upon the Marriage Bond. It is in no way comparable to the functioning of the officers of the Catholic Matrimonial Tribunal. These officers have no authority over the Bond of Marriage but are trained to examine the evidence which may make it certain that no sacred bond has ever been assumed by the parties to the civil contract. The two procedures have no relationship to each other.

The civil court takes action to determine the ensuing civil status of each member of the family; the Matrimonial Tribunal examines the evidence and answers "yes" or "no" as to a fact. For example:

The children of a divorced Catholic couple are placed by the civil court in the status of the children of a civil marriage; the *fact*, however, remains that they are born of a marriage which did not exist. And so it goes with all the details of separation.

When a Catholic couple has sought and obtained a civil divorce without consulting their own Matrimonial Tribunal, that very fact gives a hint of the possibility that their understanding of the nature of Catholic Marriage was so defective that they were really and truly incapable of conferring the Sacrament upon each other. The entire history, then, of their marriage and their previous lives, may be examined as to the evidence of this possibility.

This evidence of nullity is obviously immensely varied. It is a rapidly expanding area of Church law and jurisprudence. There is a *Handbook of Marriage Cases* prepared for the officers of the Canadian Regional Tribunals which contains 172 pages of material discussing these variations. The Introduction contains the following sentence:

> "Those preparing nullity cases on any level must surely become increasingly aware of their role in safeguarding the sacred bond of marriage, where such a bond exists in fact, while at the same time bringing the healing compassion of Christ to all without exception, who ask their help."

Some of the sources of nullity are: previous married state of either or both spouses, mental illness, force and fear (e.g. a pregnant woman seeking protection), homosexuality, non-consummation of marriage, non-baptism, provable intention to practice contraception, age below the legal requirement, schizophrenia, alcoholism before marriage, lack of due discretion or insight as to the meaning of marriage. This last source of nullity also has endless variations and psychiatric connotations.

If you are a divorced Catholic person or, if separation seems inevitable, you need have no hesitation in going to the Chancery Office of your Diocese and asking for help from an officer of the Matrimonial Tribunal. But, never under any circumstances, anticipate a decree of nullity in your relations with the opposite sex.

CHAPTER XVII
GOD'S LOVE OFFERS PEACE AND JOY TO EVERYONE

During my entire life as a priest I have marveled with increasing amazement at the fine-edged precision with which God manages, hour by hour, every tiny event in the world's progress. The result is an ever-manifest *perfect* unfolding of His plan for the everlasting welfare of all the souls who do not close their wills to the acceptance of His love.

And the most amazing feature of it all is that He uses every act of the will of every individual without the slightest compulsion of that will at any time. The thoughts of hate and malice and lust are allowed to develop into evil acts just as readily as the thoughts of love and praise and thanks are allowed to use the grace offered by God to develop into the precious acts of good will toward God and man. And all combine to produce unbelievable perfection out of what sometimes seems to be unbelievable turmoil and evil.

All this has come to my mind today as a result of one tiny item of it that happened yesterday. A question was asked of me by a guest at Westminster Abbey which reminded me of a paragraph I read last November in a little magazine of the Franciscan Fathers called *Focus*. I remember it because it quoted the following paragraph from one of my books written several years ago:

"In my own life all anxiety for the future or perplexity in the present have practically vanished from my thoughts. They are replaced by a confidence that knows for certain that every detail that unfolds, day by day, and hour by hour, is a part of the mosaic of my life that is composed by God with divine perfection. The result is a peace of soul and an enthusiasm for work which would be impossible in any human circumstances of life howsoever consoling they might be."

That tiny happening of yesterday is a first class example of God's neat way of promoting His plan. He gave me that nudge to prod me into writing about a subject that has puzzled me for several years.

How was it possible for the Crucifixion of Almighty God to come about? There was only a hairs' breadth of difference between the events which led to the Crucifixion of Jesus Christ and those events going on at the same time which almost made Him the triumphant King of the Jewish Nation and the God-Founder of the Christian Church of those whom God had chosen long before to bring salvation to the world.

Jesus Christ had to be extremely careful in everything He said and did to avoid being made King instead of allowing the jealous hate of a handful of those in the Sanhedrin to bring about His Crucifixion and to do their best to suppress the results of the Resurrection.

As a matter of fact, death by crucifixion was beyond the power of those in the Sanhedrin to bring about. But God, to achieve His purpose, used their hatred to show as evidence of political defection and gave Pontius Pilate, who acted through fear, occasion to give the necessary edict of condemnation. Thus the Crucifixion was actually carried out by Roman authority as punishment of a crime allegedly committed by Christ against Roman Law.

But why, in all the past two thousand years, has not the deep Faith of the Jewish People reversed that hairs' breadth of difference between political and religious motivation? The answer: God's *perfect* plan called for what actually happened.

The Jewish people were chosen by God to present His love and the worship due to Him, to all the

God's Love Offers Peace and Joy to Everybody 177

world. The Crucifixion, suffered for the sin of all men of all time, was God's choice of the way to make the immensity of His love known to all the men of the future. The immediate compelling acceptance of the Messiah by all the Jews would have tended to confine the establishment of His Mystical Body on earth to His own persecuted Nation. The Crucifixion tore open the Gates of Heaven and placed an obstacle of Divine Love before the Gates of Hell. All the world was thus invited to join God's Chosen Race in adoring love and worship.

Jesus Christ knew exactly what to do and say to bring about the Crucifixion *without* compulsion of any man's will. And the same is true of God's management of all the history of Christianity since the Resurrection.

But the most precious aspect of it all is that He brought about His own Crucifixion as a criminal and still left sufficient evidence that it was brought about by His love, to make thousands of Gentiles, together with the Jews who believed in His love, willing to face torture and death rather than yield to the determined zeal of those responsible for the Crucifixion to make them deny Him.

There again, the hairs' breadth precision of the evidence produced exactly the results that God had planned. God saw to it that the members of the Sanhedrin were the very first to have the all-but-compelling evidence of the Resurrection placed before them. Their own paid guards at the mouth of the tomb were the actual witnesses of the opening of the tomb by an angel while an earthquake insured their wakefulness. These guards hastened to give them this evidence in the middle of the night. And they, in abject fear of immediate stoning by the sorrowing multitude, copiously bribed their guards to swear to the story that the cowering and terrified

Apostles, locked in the upper room in fear, had come and robbed the tomb and concealed the crucified body of Him in whom they had placed their hopes.

It must be admitted, however, that the falsity of this story that saved the lives of the crucifiers is far more apparent today than it was when it was first concocted. And there again, the nicety of God's management allowed enough acceptance to save the lives of the bribers and not enough to bring about the extermination of the little group of believers as the bribers had hoped.

Furthermore, their knowledge that the Resurrection had taken place, determined their behavior for the rest of their lives. It made them afraid to launch an immediate attack and permitted the amazing survival of the Church which would have been utterly impossible if their story had been true.

But what has all this ancient history to do with my admiration of God's perfect management of the results of the thoughts and words and acts of every individual soul in the world today? It has everything to do with it! It shows that God has provided evidence recorded in the New Testament which He has almost miraculously guarded from destruction until the present day. This evidence is presented in a way that provides two indirect proofs *sufficient* to make it altogether reasonable to believe that the Resurrection took place and that it proved the Divinity of Christ.

First: Imagine that the story spread abroad by the guards at the Holy Sepulcher, was true and not a richly bribed lie. Can you think of any possible reason which would have prevented the leaders of the Sanhedrin from rounding up every member of Christ's company and stoning them if they refused to produce the Body?

Second: Can you think of any possible reason why

God's Love Offers Peace and Joy to Everybody 179

the Apostles would have faced the torture and death that was eventually meeted out to them, instead of producing the Body, when all their hopes had failed and they had, as a last resort, stolen the Body and fabricated the story of the Resurrection?

There *is* no answer to either question and I am beginning to wonder if perhaps God is allowing the intolerable heresy and apostasy among the priests of the Church today, to remind the Jews of those two unanswerable questions and make them realize how they have been robbed of the prestige and honor that God would offer them if they would enrich their present religion with the worship of *their* Jewish Messiah!

The lovely Jewess, Our Lady of Fatima, has put these thoughts in my mind as I have been reading her words in the little book: *Our Lady Speaks to Her Beloved Priests*. For the past seven years she has been giving messages of love and encouragement to those Catholic priests who refuse to accept the heresies of today and who remain loyal to the Holy Father.

Our Lady has been very specific in directing the recipient of these messages. Her words have given such clear evidence of authenticity that they have gained acceptance throughout the world and, with amazing force, since 1972, have brought about *The Marian Movement of Priests* consecrated to her Immaculate Heart. She speaks with such confidence and authority that acceptance of her loving leadership becomes automatic.

Her book is addressed directly to the Catholic priests who will form her cohort to save the Catholic Church from the final assault of Satan, but it invites the attention of every human being in the world. It somehow makes me think that it will eventually help the Jews to believe that the centuries of build-up of evidence for the Resurrection of Jesus Christ mark Him as their Messiah and that He may bring it all to a show-down soon.

Obviously, the Jews who practice their ancient religion today, are definitely not disposed to accept a message said to be given by the Mother of Jesus of Nazareth to a Catholic priest in the 1970's. It is equally obvious that neither they nor other non-practicing members of the Jewish Race will be reading this book in great numbers. So, since this chapter is really written to help strengthen the Faith of Catholics in these days of wholesale apostasy, it is worth while to quote the words of Our Lady of Fatima to the recipient of her messages, Rev. Don Stefano Gobbi, of Milan, Italy on Christmas Eve, 1975.

As a matter of fact, her messages would be of interest and deep concern to every Jew in the world. So it just might happen that God, in His perfect management of all things, would maneuver a miracle so that ten million Jews would read it. In that case, there might be ten million more Rosaries prayed every day. Then Russia could not hold out for long!

Here is the message. Let's pray that the Jews *will* read it and then read the rest of the book:

(Holy Night)   December 24, 1975

"Do not fear: This night is the Holy Night. Live it in my heart, my beloved sons.

I want to make you share in all my love, in my maternal anxiety at the moment when, in a ravishing celestial light my Son, Jesus is born into the world. He is born of me, His Mother, in a virginal and miraculous way.

It was deep night. Deeper still was the night that enveloped humanity, enslaved in sin and with no further hope of salvation. . . . During this night so deep, the Light appeared, my little Infant was born, at a time when

God's Love Offers Peace and Joy to Everybody 181

no one expected Him and when there was no place to receive Him.

Unexpected, unwelcomed, rejected by humanity; and yet, my Jesus is born to redeem all mankind from their sins.

It is in this way that the Light appeared amid such darkness, and my little Child came to save the world.

He is born in poverty and in the pain of rejection, and His first wailings were only tears. He feels the rigor of the cold at the same time that the coldness of mankind envelops Him.

My Immaculate Heart gathered the first tears of the Divine Infant. They mixed with those of my Heart and I wiped them away with my motherly kisses.

On this holy night, at the moment when I again give you my Son, I say to you once more: Do not fear: Jesus is your Savior.

Now, more than ever, the world is plunged in darkness: the coldness of hatred, of pride, and of doubt envelopes the hearts of men. The Church also is disrupted by a profound crisis: even many of His priests have doubts about my little Infant.

O my Church, receive with joy the coming of your Jesus: He lives in you because He wishes to save all my poor sons!

Priests consecrated to my Immaculate Heart, *do not fear*. Today I announce to you a great news that is a joy for every one: my Son, Jesus, is your Savior. You were all redeemed by Him; now you can be saved by Him.

Do not fear: just as my Heart gave you a Savior, so now in these times my Immaculate Heart gives you the joy of His Salvation.

Soon, the whole world, invaded by darkness and snatched from my Son, will finally rejoice over the fruit of this holy night.

The triumph of my Immaculate Heart will be realized through a new birth of Jesus in the hearts and in the souls of my poor lost sons.

Only have trust and you will never be overwhelmed by anxiety or discouragement. The future that awaits you will be a new dawn of Light for the whole world henceforth purified.

During this night, close by the poor crib of my Child, I feel the loving presence of my beloved sons, priests consecrated to my Immaculate Heart, and with my Son, Jesus, whom I clasp to my Heart, I thank you all and I bless you."

It does indeed appear that God is allowing the present surge of evil in the Church and Our Lady's sadness as she clasps her Son, Jesus, to her Heart, to shout aloud God's message to all who do not deliberately close their wills against Him. If God brought this message to the Jews of today, it might make them look at their present status in the light of the history of their Nation from its very beginning.

The Hebrew Scriptures are saturated with evidence that the final stages of God's eternal plan for the consummation of His love for man should be brought to the whole world through His Chosen Race. From God's summons to Abraham to come out of the East, until the present day, God has preserved the chain of continuity against what has been the perversity of a few of their leaders.

After the punishment of their slavery in Egypt, God rescued them in a manner which should have given eternal certainty that God was their Savior and the Director of their destiny. But all too soon, they seemed to forget and defy God's commands. So, God led them through an amazing history of punishment, repentance, forgiveness, devotion—followed by defection and betrayal of God's love. Before Christ came into the world, their defection was usually into idolatry copied from their neighbors. But the Crucifixion of Christ left those who accepted the lie of their leaders, still hoping for a Messiah who would fulfill all the promises made to them by God.

God's Love Offers Peace and Joy to Everybody 183

The situation today, however, if viewed by Jew or Atheist or Christian, with an honest effort to quench *a priori* prejudice, continues to display God's ingenuity in devising ways to bring about acceptance by the Jews of the all-but-unbelievable demonstration of the love of the God-Man who was crucified and rose from the dead, as the glorious fruition of their Faith.

In view of the two questions proposed above, the survival of Christianity would have been impossible if the Resurrection was a fraud. And with the Resurrection as an accepted truth, it is equally impossible to deny Christ as the Messiah of the Jews. God, as always, is certainly inviting the Jews to recognize their *rights* as Founders of Christianity. And Saint Peter was bold enough to challenge the crucifiers of Christ as to those very rights when he addressed the Sanhedrin after Christ's Ascension into heaven:

> "The God of our Fathers has raised up Jesus whom you put to death, hanging Him on a tree. He whom God has exalted at His right hand as Ruler and Savior, is to bring repentance to Israel and forgiveness of sins. We testify to this: so too does the Holy Spirit, whom God has given to those who obey Him." (Acts 5:30-32).

Saul of Tarsus was perhaps the outstanding stalwart among the Hebrews who refused to tolerate the thought that Jesus Christ was the *kind* of Messiah whom God had promised for the fulfillment of the religion He had given them. And yet God chose him and smote him with a miracle of grace to learn that Christ, during His entire sojourn on earth, precisely fulfilled the words of the prophets recorded in the Hebrew Scriptures to expand their worship with an outpouring of divine love and an invitation to the whole world to share in their worship and His love.

In Saint Paul's Epistle to the Romans, Chapters 9

to 11, Saint Paul explains this mission of his apostolate as follows:

> "I am not deceiving you, I am telling you the truth in Christ's name, with the full assurance of a conscience enlightened by the Holy Spirit, when I tell you of the great sorrow, the continual anguish I feel in my heart, and how it has ever been my wish that I myself might be doomed to separation from Christ, if that would benefit my brethren, my own kinsmen by race. They are Israelites, adopted as God's sons: the visible presence, and the covenant, and the giving of the law, and the Temple Worship, and the promises, are their inheritance; the patriarchs belong to them, and theirs is the human stock from which Christ came; Christ who rules as God over all things blessed for ever. Amen. And yet it is not as if God's promise had failed of its effect." (9:1–6).
> "We are the object of God's mercy; we whom He has called, Jews and Gentiles alike." (Acts 9:24)

> "Brethren, they have all the good will of my heart, all my prayers to God for their salvation. That they are jealous for God's honor, I can testify; but it is with imperfect understanding. They did not recognize God's way of justification, and so they tried to institute a way of their own, instead of submitting to His. Christ has superceded the law, bringing justification to anyone who will believe." (10:1–4). "Thou canst find salvation, if thou wilt use thy lips to confess that Jesus is the Lord, and thy heart to believe that God has raised Him up from the dead. The heart has only to believe, if we are to be justified; the lips have only to make confession, if we are to be saved. That is what Scripture says, Anyone who believes in Him will not be disappointed." (10:9–11).

> "Tell me, then, has God disowned His people? That is not to be thought of. Why, I am an Israelite myself, descended from Abraham; Benjamin is my tribe. No, God has not disowned the people which, from the first, He recognized as His." (11:1–2). "So it is our time; a remnant has remained true; grace has chosen it. And if it is due to grace, then it is not due to observance of the law; if it were, grace would be no grace at all. What does it

God's Love Offers Peace and Joy to Everybody 185

mean, then? Why, that Israel has missed the mark; only this chosen remnant has attained it, while the rest were blinded; so we read in the scriptures, God has numbed their senses, given them unseeing eyes and deaf ears, to this day." (11:5–8). "Tell me, then, have they stumbled so as to fall altogether? God forbid; the result of their false step has been to bring the Gentiles salvation, and the results of that must be to rouse the Jews to emulate them." (11:11). "Blindness has fallen upon a part of Israel, but only until the tale of the Gentile nations is complete; then the whole of Israel will find salvation, as we read in scripture, A deliverer shall come from Sion, to rid Jacob of his unfaithfulness; and this shall be the fulfillment of My covenant with them when I take away their sins." (11:25–27).

If a considerable percentage of the Jews would recognize their rightful status now, it would almost certainly cause the tragedy of a divided Christendom to be recognized throughout the world. And if *that* happened, the *a priori* closed will of Atheism would meet with devastating scrutiny.

Again, looked at from the viewpoint of cold reason, the survival and even rapid increase of the number of victims of Atheism, is the most amazing achievement of Satan in the history of the world. It is the outstanding evidence of the deceiving power of wholesale example to triumph over reason. There is not now, and there never has been, a sound basis of reason to sustain the claim of Atheism. Entirely aside from any supernatural evidence or any revelation, the self-existence of matter cannot be defended by reason. Existence of matter, whether eternal or temporal, demands a Source of Power to exist that can bring being out of nothing, and that means creation.

I am told that Saint Thomas Aquinas affirmed that revelation was needed to *prove* creation. But the vastly enlarged knowledge of the nature of matter as a manifestation of energy, removes that need as of today and allows reason alone to prove the fallacy of the claim of the possibility of the self existence of eternal matter.

To make the obvious a little more concrete, imagine a glass globe of any dimension, enclosing a total vacuum. In order to affirm the possibility of the self existence of matter taking place in this globe, it must be assumed to have a power to bring itself into existence out of nothing. But if that "IT" were present, there is not a perfect vacuum. We must repeat; the existence of matter demands a Source of Power capable of bringing existence out of *nothing*.

Now, to amplify the example, imagine the globe extended to infinity and enduring from eternity; then remove the globe and repeat the paragraph above. The *"Big Bang"* theory demands the same "IT" which does not exist, to operate the *Bang*.

To resort to "eternal matter" to remove the obvious impossibility of self generation without a Source, is equivalent to soothing a child frightened by a nightmare by opening a window and throwing the fiend out and closing the window.

And, if it is argued that the claim of the Source of creation is no more compelling to reason than is the claim of "eternal matter"; then the infinite complexity and perfection of the ultimate fruit of eternal matter overwhelmingly excludes the possibility of unguided evolution. In addition to the necessity of a Source of mere existence, being alive and being aware of existence and having intelligence, are each equally demanding of a Source beyond the nature of existence itself.

There are billions of items of evidence of the demand for creative guidance in evolution. One of a purely material nature that I have used elsewhere in my writing, is the possession of the human eye. Without creation of the eye, we must postulate the self-

God's Love Offers Peace and Joy to Everybody 187

generation of some fourteen capacities as a result of light shining on living matter and then assume that they find each other and unite before any result is achieved.

I have on my desk an amusing little tract entitled: *The Non-Evolution of the Bombardier Beetle*, authored by Dr. Duane T. Gish and related by him at a Summer Institute of Scientific Creationism at Joplin, Missouri, in June, 1976. The tract opens with the following paragraph.

> "A German chemist undertook the investigation of the bombardier beetle. He found that the bombardier beetle has twin storage chambers, twin combustion tubes and in these tubes he stores a mixture of hydrogen peroxide and hydrogen quinone. Now, this is an explosive reaction mixture. If you or I went into the laboratory and mixed these two chemicals, the mixture would explode in our faces. But the bombardier beetle adds an *inhibitor* which prevents the explosion. And then, when an enemy approaches him, he squirts this solution into the twin combustion chambers and—just at the right moment—he adds an *anti*-inhibitor, and BOOM! it explodes in the face of his enemy."

The tract then continues with amusing illustrations and comments to show how the possession of these lethal weapons would annihilate the possessor at each stage of acquisition until he had all of them *and* the know-how to use them. Near the end of the tract, there are the following paragraphs:

> "Please note, too, that what is here is much more than a classic bit of evolutionary satire. It is really a *proof*—a proof from *reason*—that evolution is false and Creation is true.
>
> "Evolution is said to work by *processes* leading up to organized and more highly organized *products*. But such is clearly impossible because the processes themselves cannot produce the product of which they are a part.

Evolution has everything *backwards*. The completed product *must* come *first*.

"And this is what God creates. He creates products. The little bombardier beetle is a proof positive of Creation!"

I recommend to every professed Atheist that he order a copy of this tract from: Catholic Center for Creation Research, 1122 Garvin Place #113, Louisville, Kentucky 40203, and wear it close to his heart!

Then, let the Atheist and Jew and Christian make a copy of Psalm 32:8-15 and wear it close to our hearts.

"Let all the earth fear the Lord, all who live in the world revere Him.

He spoke; and it came to be. He commanded; it sprang into being.

He frustrates the designs of the nations, He defeats the plans of the peoples.

His own designs shall stand forever, the plans of His heart from age to age.

They are happy whose God is the Lord, the people He has chosen as His own.

From the heavens the Lord looks forth, He sees all the children of men.

From the place where He dwells, He gazes on all the dwellers on the earth,

He who shapes the hearts of them all, and considers all their deeds."

Yes, His own designs shall stand for ever. God is inviting mankind to heal the setting for disaster that faces man today but He will never compel man's will. God manages everything *perfectly*. He offers us *peace* with His guidance, or self-inflicted disaster without Him—man must choose!

And to help our choice, let us listen to the words of the Mystic Gabrielle Bossis reported in that priceless little story: *He & I*, published by Editions Paul-

God's Love Offers Peace and Joy to Everybody

ines, Sherbrooke, Quebec. Jesus speaks to her in these words:

"I lived so strenuously—I was going to say, so painfully—for you. Then you can understand, can't you, how deeply I long for the loving response of your life. I have an absolute need for the return-sacrifice of your body, and much more, of your faculties that you received from Me. Above all, of your thoughts; they move your heart and make you act for Me. Your thoughts can lay hold of Me and keep Me and they are proof to Me of you. They can lead you to heroism and enable you to put Me on as raiment that fits you in every detail. And when your thoughts reach Me, joyous because they are tender, what wouldn't I give you for their confidence!"

OTHER FINE BOOKS

By: Father Bede Reynolds, O.S.B.

If you liked this book, then you must read the entire series of which it forms part.

- **A REBEL FROM RICHES** tells Fr. Bede's own life story and makes you his close friend.
- **HOW COME MY FAITH?** offers a practical foundation for sound Christian living
- **PROJECT SAINTHOOD, YOUR BUSINESS** puts HOW COME into action.
- **LET'S MEND THE MESS**, as you have now seen, enlists the widest possible support in the struggle against modern foes of the Church.
- **DRAW YOUR STRENGTH FROM THE LORD** Fr. Bede knows that those who dedicate themselves to an enterprise of this magnitude need much spiritual nourishment to keep them going.

These five books are intended to urge all men and women to turn away from Satan and return to sanity and sanctity. Already they have achieved just that for thousands and now YOU have been contacted, through the zeal of Fr. Bede and the goodness of God, and invited to do YOUR part.

The books may be ordered from the publisher, from Fr. Bede in Westminster Abbey, Mission City, B.C. Canada or from THE RIEHLE FOUNDATION, P.O. Box 7, Milford, Ohio, 45150, a non-profit corporation formed for the explicit purpose of promoting these ideals.

COMMENTS FROM READERS

"Congratulations on the success of your new book, *How Come My Faith?* which I found very inspirational, and the fact that you are a convert, lived a worldly life, and were happily married, gives the reader much 'food for thought.'"

"My thanks for your book carries with it my congratulations on this work, which reflects your experience, your zeal and your prayers for God's holy Church. I am reading it with admiration for the literary style as well as for the good solid Catholic content."
"I liked very much the way you portrayed *Mass, grace* and *death.* It is by far the best book in concise size that I have read in many years. I like *Rebel From Riches* too: it's a masterpiece"!

"How very pleased I was to have received your two copies of *How Come My Faith?* Perhaps unknown to us God in His master plan, arranged for the publication at this time, not sooner, not later! I believe this so strongly because, upon arrival of your two copies, two very dear friends of ours were seriously ill. One man is a fallen-away Catholic and the woman is in need of having her faith restored. Both were in the hospital, and I mailed each of them a copy of your book. Today, I heard from the lady whose comments were most gratifying. She said your book inspired her immensely and she plans to read it over again.

Your book is now most needed by many Catholics and non-Catholics. There seems to be a tremendous cry for good spiritual reading, and I for one will spread the word about *How Come My Faith?* The enclosed order for twenty copies is the start of several orders I will place."

"Congratulations on your fine masterpiece! I have enjoyed every page. I am sure that many, especially our young people will thank God for your faith and zeal."

"Father Bede sent me a copy of the manuscript of **PROJECT SAINTHOOD**. After reading it I honestly believe the book will be a bestseller, as the suggestions made by Father Bede will be a sure cure of the evils of our day. As he says, being a living saint not only solves our individual problem this minute, but solves once and for all where we are going to spend eternity.

FROM A PARISH BULLETIN: "Most of you will remember the grand old Benedictine who has helped us out during the summer months the last few years. But few will know his story. His autobiography—A REBEL FROM RICHES—is now available in the book rack. It is a heart-warming story of a successful business career, happiness in marriage, the life and death of Patty, his wife, and within three months the give-away and the contemplative life as a son of Saint Benedict. It is a book you will enjoy reading and will like to pass on to your friends. It could be a means of grace for many."

"Your book is really a tonic for those who are groping their way through a world of violence and tension and misunderstanding, for it speaks truly of the love of God, both in His human and Divine dimensions. I congratulate you on this happy type of authorship."

"My evaluation of your book is that it is an intensely personal and deeply moving book which reads so smoothly and really reaches out to the reader in such a way that the reader is inspired, challenged, and left with the conviction that the author is indeed GOD'S MESSENGER in a world that needs so much more of the same type of book."

"Here's proof that your book has a UNIVERSAL APPEAL. I cherished it as a love story with a spiritual background; my husband found your business experiences most interesting; my fourteen-year-old son was keen to read it as an adventure story."

"I can't begin to tell you how much I enjoyed this book. It is delightfully written and a very thrilling story. It should be a 'best-seller' overnight"!

If you have found enlightenment through this book, why not share it with a friend, a neighbor, a casual acquaintance, somebody you met by chance?

Or maybe you, or somebody you know, might like to use books like this one, and similar methods, to tell people about the Lord? If so, then you should contact the Society of St. Paul (Alba House Communications), a group of religious men who dedicate themselves to bringing the message of Christ to others through the media of communication while living the religious life.

Write today to the Vocation Office, Society of St. Paul, Canfield, Ohio 44406, or to Vocation Office, Society of St. Paul, 2187 Victory Blvd., Staten Island, N.Y. 10314.